D!RTY

SPANISH
WORKBOOK

D!RTY®
SPANISH WORKBOOK

101 Fun Exercises Filled with Slang, Sex and Swearing

NDB

illustrated by **LINDSAY MACK**

ULYSSES PRESS

Published by:
Ulysses Press
P.O. Box 3440
Berkeley, CA 94703
www.ulyssespress.com

ISBN: 978-1-56975-928-8
Library of Congress Control Number: 2012937122

Printed in the United States

10 9 8 7 6 5 4 3 2 1

Acquisitions editor: Keith Riegert
Managing editor: Claire Chun
Spanish editor: Dana Montoro
English editor: Lauren Harrison
Project editor: Alice Riegert
Production: Abigail Reser, Jake Flaherty
Original series cover design: Double R Design
Front cover photos: mariachi © Alija/istockphoto.com; Mexican doll © Nino_Cavalier/istockphoto.com;
        woman © FernandoAH/istockphoto.com
Back cover illustration: Lindsay Mack

Please note: *Dirty Spanish Workbook* is a work of parody in book format. No affiliation with, and no sponsorship or endorsement by celebrities who are parodied in this work is claimed or suggested.

The author would like to dedicate this book to his grandmother for her dirty sense of humor and to his mother for making him spend six weeks in Mexico when he was 15 and just wanted to stay home to play video games and make out with his girlfriend all summer. That trip was formative and that girlfriend sucked. Nice work, Mom.

TABLE OF CONTENTS

·····Acknowledgments

The author would like to thank Alice Riegert of Ulysses Press for putting up with the author while he missed deadlines and ignored her e-mails. She gave good feedback and never got upset. Thanks Alice.

Acknowledgment and appreciation goes to Juan Caballero for blazing the trail in the original *Dirty Spanish* phrasebook.

Large thanks are also due to the good people on the forums of WordReference.com. Tons of knowledge and resources on there about slang from countries all over the world. Keep up the good work.

And lastly, thanks in advance to the Pulitzer and Nobel committees for choosing my little book for their respective awards. I plan to be humbled by your eventual acknowledgment.

USING THIS WORKBOOK

A couple of things to note before you dive in here. First of all, this is a workbook, not a phrasebook. The purpose of a workbook is to help you really learn something, like embed-it-in-your-thick-brain learn, not just see a word once and forget about it, which is how most of us went through our high school Spanish classes. Because what's the point of learning the phrase "Go fuck yourself" if you can't remember how to say it when it really matters?

So this workbook is designed to give you opportunities to put your new Spanish skillz to use so you actually remember what to say when it counts. But to really get good you have to practice in the real world, too. So go to your mom and call her a *gran puta vieja*, ask your boss if he wants a *puñetazo*, and tell your girlfriend that she's been slacking in the *mamada* department or your boyfriend that he needs to *comer la concha* more. These are the sorts of real-world scenarios that'll make you a slang expert!

You should also know that this book is written under the assumption that you already know at least some basic Spanish. If not, no biggie. You'll still be able to learn a bunch of cool-ass words. But you'll get a lot more out of it if you have a foundation to start from. If you're looking for a basic primer on Spanish, however, this is not the book for you. I repeat: Step away from this book. This is not the place to learn how to say, "Excuse me, sir, where is the library?" or, "I live in the house that is big and red," or, "I have 15 years, and you?" If, on the other hand, you are looking to learn how to say, "Raul is a fucking cocksucker," or, "Your mom has some giant-ass titties," then welcome, you've come to the right place!

Throughout the book, you'll notice that some of the Spanish words are given with variations or alternative endings (e.g., *gordo*/a or *tu/s*). That's to denote gender or plural differences. Again, we're assuming that (a) you already have some basic Spanish under your belt and (b) you're not a fucking moron, so you should be able to figure it out. If you're really mystified and you actually care to know the difference, a quick Google search on Spanish grammar or an actual grammar workbook should set you straight.

Obviously, Spanish is spoken in a lot of different countries (21 if you include Puerto Rico—thanks, Wikipedia!). Each country has slightly different slang. The classic example is the word *coger*. In Spain, *coger* means "to take," as in "to take the bus." In Mexico though, *coger* means "to fuck," as in "to fuck your best friend's mom." The words chosen for this workbook, however, are the ones most universally recognized across countries. So for the most part you'll be safe using this vocab from Spain and Mexico all the way to Argentina. And by "safe" I mean that people will understand them, not "safe" as in free from bodily harm, since about 95 percent of the words in here could get your ass beat if used in the wrong situation.

Now go forward, young grasshopper. I have much to teach you. Take your Spanish and get very, very dirty with it.

Pronunciation guide

Speaking Spanish like a gringo is one of the least cool things I can imagine. So turn on a *telenovela* on Univision and pay attention to the way they talk. Doesn't matter if you can't understand a word they're saying. Just listen to the rhythm and inflection of their speech. And while you're there, you might as well check out the racks on their soap stars. They're amazing! But back to the speech.

WATCH YOUR VOWELS

Spanish vowels sound very different from English vowels. Take the letter "a" for instance. They never sound like the hard "a" in "gay" or the long "a" in "apple." They always sound like the "ahhh" sound in "water." Use this chart below to help.

A is like the "au" in "naughty."

E is like the "e" in "wet" if at the beginning of a word and like the "a" in "gay" if at the end of a word.

I is like the "ee" in "weed."

O is like the "o" in "bone."

U is like the "oo" in "poon."

PAY ATTENTION TO ACCENTS

Most Spanish words stress the next-to-last syllable unless an accent mark notes otherwise. So for instance the word for "we hooked up" is *ligamos*. It's pronounced leeh-GAH-mos with the stress on the next to last syllable (i.e., the second syllable in this case). It's not LEE-ga-mos with the stress on the first syllable. It's leeh-GAH-mos.

If you see an accent mark, however, be sure to stress that sound in the word. Take the word *acción*. There are three syllables, ahk-seen-OHN, with the stress on the final syllable with the "o." You would not say ahk-SEE-ohn.

The only other time the next-to-last-syllable rule doesn't apply is with verbs in the infinitive (*comer*, *jugar*, etc.). With these words, the stress falls on the last syllable.

And finally, don't worry so much about saying something wrong that you're too afraid to talk. That's the biggest mistake people make when they learn a language. You can't make an omelet without cracking a few eggs. You're going to make mistakes. Get over it. Think of each mistake as an opportunity to learn. You should go out of your way to talk to people that you don't even need to just as an opportunity to practice. And luckily for you, Spanish speakers tend to be a pretty friendly bunch who are easy to talk to. Now quit being a pussy and go talk to some people!

CHAPTER 1

FRIENDLY SPANISH
ESPAÑOL AMIGUERO

Spanish speakers are generally a friendly bunch, quick to welcome you in and treat you like part of the fam. But once you're in, you gotta know how to drop the formalities and talk like you're part of the crew rather than some random outsider. Nobody says *¿Cómo está, usted?* to anybody they know or like. Ya gotta keep it chill.

•••••What's up?

Greetings are the bread and butter of building good relationships. Master the phrases below so you don't sound like some uptight tool with a stick up your ass. You wanna come off as smooth and relaxed. Keep in mind that in most situations, guys and girls will kiss hello with a quick air-kiss on the cheek. Sometimes guys will do this too (and it's not considered gay), but more often than not it's just a shake of the hands.

SLANG BOX

GREETING		RESPONSES	
What's your name?	*¿Cómo te llamas?*	My name is . . .	*Me llamo . . .*
What's up?	*¿Qué tal?*	Everything's good.	*Todo bien.*
What's happenin'?	*¿Qué pasó?*	I'm all right.	*Ando ahí nomás.*
Whatcha up to?	*¿Qué haces?*	Straight chillin'.	*Todo tranqui'.*
What's the word?	*¿Qué dices?*	Same as ever.	*Como siempre.*
What'd I miss?	*¿Quihubo?*	Nothin' much.	*No mucho.*
How's everything?	*¿Cómo va todo?*		
How you been doing?	*¿Cómo andas?*		
Everything good?	*¿Todo bien?*		

Exercise 1.1   Makin' small talk

Fill in the blanks of this stuttering conversation so our young Romeo can get his pole greased by his sweet Juliet.

Hola, ¿Cómo te _____?

_____ llamo Julieta.

¿_____ pasó, Julieta? Soy Romeo.

Como _____ Romeo. ¿Y _____? ¿_____ andas?

Todo _____, mamacita.

Exercise 1.2   Call and response

Write an appropriate response based on the given greeting.

1. *¿Qué haces?*   Response: _____

2. *¿Quihubo?*   Response: _____

3. *¿Todo bien?*   Response: _____

4. *¿Cómo andas?*   Response: _____

5. *¿Qué pasa?*   Response: _____

Now write an appropriate greeting based on the response given.

6. Greeting: _____   *Todo bien.*

7. Greeting: _____   *Como siempre.*

8. Greeting: _____   *Todo tranqui'.*

9. Greeting: _____   *No mucho.*

10. Greeting: _____   *Ando ahí nomás.*

Exercise 1.3 Dr. Conversation

Fix each convo by putting it in the appropriate order.

1.   a. *No mucho. ¿Y tu?*   _____

      b. *¿Qué tal?*   _____

      c. *Todo bien.*   _____

2.   a. *Ando ahí nomás.*   _____

      b. *Todo tranqui'. ¿Qué pasa contigo?*   _____

      c. *¿Qué haces?*   _____

3.   a. *¿Qué dices?*   _____

      b. *Como siempre. ¿Cómo va todo?*   _____

      c. *Ando ahí nomás.*   _____

4.   a. *Nada. Todo bien. ¿Qué haces?*   _____

      b. *Como siempre.*   _____

      c. *¿Quihubo? ¿Cómo andas?*   _____

·····Later!

Now that you got your greetings down, you gotta make sure you can peace out appropriately too. Remember that when you leave a get-together in most Spanish-speaking lands, you gotta go around and say bye to pretty much everybody in the same way that you said hello (air-kiss on the cheek for girls, handshakes for the dudes).

SLANG BOX

Later	*Chao*	**See ya 'round**	*Ahí nos vemos*
Peace	*Me largo*	**We're outta here**	*Nos huimos*
See ya later	*Hasta luego*	**Good-bye**	*Adiós*

Exercise 1.4 Choose your *adiós*

Choose the correct response based on the phrase given.

1. Necesito ir.
   a. Me largo.
   b. Tu madre.
   c. ¿Qué tal?

2. Tu madre es una puta gorda.
   a. Ahí nos vemos.
   b. Hasta luego.
   c. ¡Cierra la boca, bastardo!

3. Nos huimos.
   a. ¿Qué pasa?
   b. ¿Cómo andas?
   c. Chao.

4. ¿Quieres tener sexo?
   a. ¡Sí!
   b. ¡No!
   c. Ahí nos vemos.

5. Hasta luego.
   a. ¿Qué dices?
   b. Me largo.
   c. Ando ahí nomás.

Exercise 1.5 Dr. Conversation *part dos*

Fix the following convos by putting them in the correct order.

1. a. Hasta luego.   _____
   b. Hola.   _____
   c. Ahí nos vemos.   _____
   d. ¿Qué tal?   _____
   e. Todo tranqui'.   _____
   f. Como siempre, ¿y tú? _____

2. a. Adiós.   _____
   b. Todo bien.   _____
   c. Ando ahí nomás. ¿Cómo va todo? _____
   d. Hasta luego.   _____
   e. ¿Como andas?   _____

3. a. No mucho. ¿Qué haces? _____
   b. Nos huimos.   _____
   c. ¿Quihubo?   _____
   d. Chao.   _____
   e. Cómo siempre.   _____

Exercise 1.6   He said/She said

Translate the introductory conversation below to see how everything works out for ol' Hernando.

·····Peeps

Hang out in Latin America long enough and you'll meet all sorts of peeps. It's important to have the vocabulary to distinguish between the randos and your inner wolf pack. Plus it's fun to be able to talk shit about all the weird people that pop up in your Facebook feed. Who the fuck are some of those douchebags?

SLANG BOX

NOUNS

Best friend	*Amigote/a*	**A dude**	*Un chavo*
My buds	*Mis cuates*	**Bro**	*'Mano*
Old school pal	*Cole*	**My boy**	*Mi compa*
Girl (youngish)	*Nena*	**My girl**	*Mi comay*
Some guy	*Algún tipo*	**The guys**	*Los muchachos*
Punk kid	*Chamaco*	**The girls**	*Las muchachas*
A chick	*Una chava*	**Good people**	*Buena gente*

Exercise 1.7   You're my boy, Blue!

Name your peeps. Fill in the blanks with someone you know personally according to how they're being described.

1. _____ es mi amigote.

2. _____ es mi cole.

3. _____ es una nena.

4. _____ es un chamaco.

5. _____ es una chava.

6. _____ es un chavo.

7. _____ es mi 'mano.

8. _____ es mi compa.

9. _____ es mi comay.

10. _____ es buena gente.

Exercise 1.8   Find-a-friend

If you can't find any amigos, *not only are you a friendless loser, but you also suck at Spanish. Sorry! Find the Spanish translations for the words below.*

1. Some guy   _____

2. My girl   _____

3. Best friend   _____

4. Good people   _____

5. A dude   _____

6. Old school pal   _____

7. A chick   _____

8. My boy   _____

9. Bro   _____

10. Girl (youngish) _____

11. Punk kid   _____

12. The guys   _____

Exercise 1.9   It's a bird! It's a plane! It's some random dude!

Circle the term that best describes the people pictured below.

1. a. Cole
   b. Nena
   c. Chamaco

2. a. Chavo
   b. Nena
   c. Muchacho

3. a. Las muchachas
   b. Buena gente
   c. Algún tipo

4. a. Chamaco
   b. Comay
   c. Compa

5. a. Un chavo
   b. Un tipo
   c. Una chava

6. a. Nena
   b. 'Mano
   c. Chamaco

7. a. Los muchachos
   b. Algún tipo
   c. Las chavas

·····Family

Ahhhhh, *la familia*. The backbone of society. The building block of humanity. The skeleton of civilization. The fountainhead of shame and sexual repression. Yes, where would we be without family? Probably living the luxuriant life we always imagined, free of guilt and crippling, pressure-induced anxiety. Family is in big in Spanish-speaking countries. Real BIG. It's not at all uncommon for multiple generations to be living under one roof together, even well after the kids are grown and have jobs of their own. Families are constantly in each other's business, but Latin Americans and Spaniards wouldn't have it any other way.

SLANG BOX

NOUNS

Daddy	*Papi*	Stepdad/Stepmom	*Padrastro/Madrastra*
Pops	*Tata*	Stepbrother/Stepsister	*Hermanastro/a*
My old man	*Mi viejo*	Stepson/Stepdaughter	*Hijastro/a*
Moms	*Mami*	Lover	*Amante*
My old woman	*Mi vieja*	Son/Daughter	*Hijo/a*
Gramps	*El abue'*	My son/daughter	*Mijo/a*
Grandma	*La abue'*	My better half	*Mi media naranja*
Bro	*'Mano*		
Sis	*'Mana*	**ADJECTIVES**	
Illegitimate son	*Hijo natural*	Married	*Casado*
		Divorced	*Divorciado*
Cuz	*Primo/a*	Remarried	*Recasado*
Uncle/Aunt	*Tío/a*	Adopted	*Adoptado*

Exercise 1.10   Your family tree

Fill in your family tree with everyone's name. Then draw a crude caricature of each member of your family in the boxes.

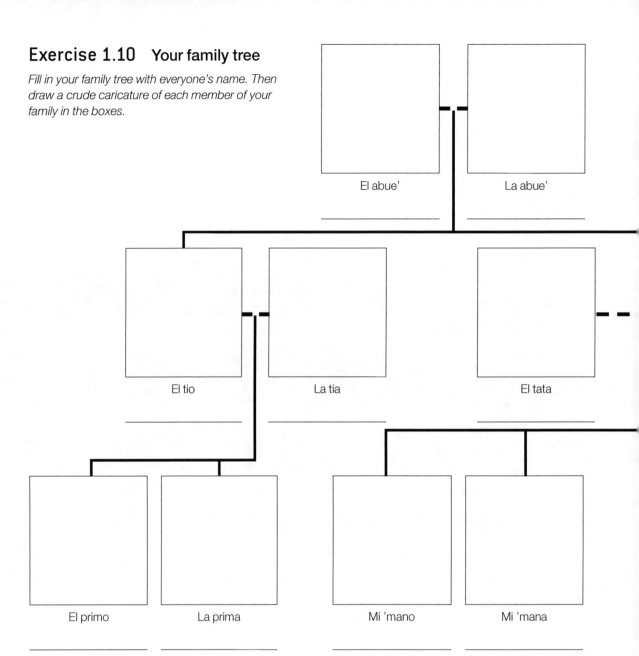

El abue'

La abue'

El tio

La tia

El tata

El primo

La prima

Mi 'mano

Mi 'mana

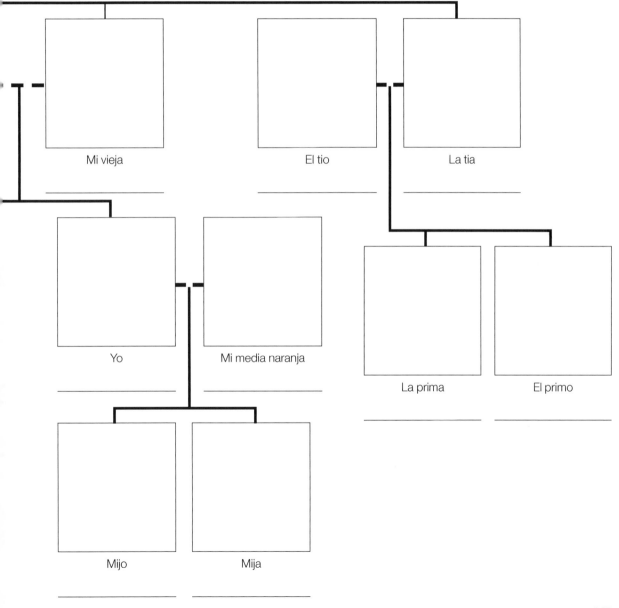

Mi vieja

El tio

La tia

Yo

Mi media naranja

La prima

El primo

Mijo

Mija

Exercise 1.11   The (modern) family tree

Label each person with the appropriate family term. You'll need to find yourself (yo) in the family tree first in order to figure out how each person is related to you.

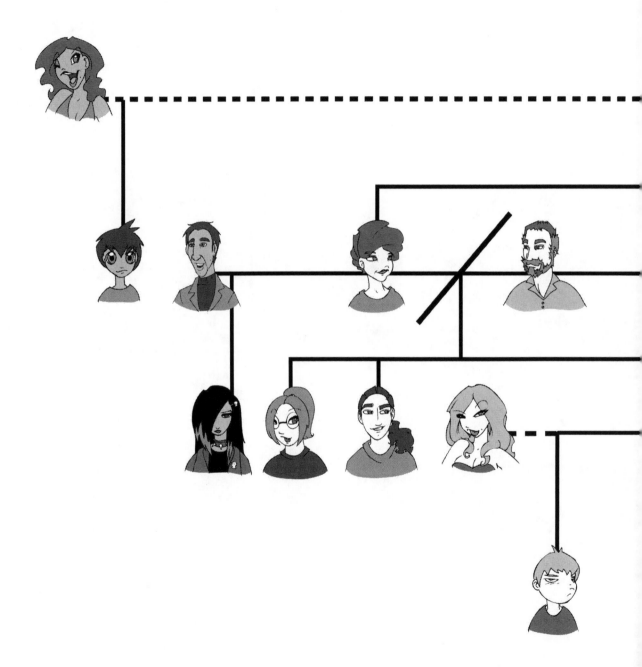

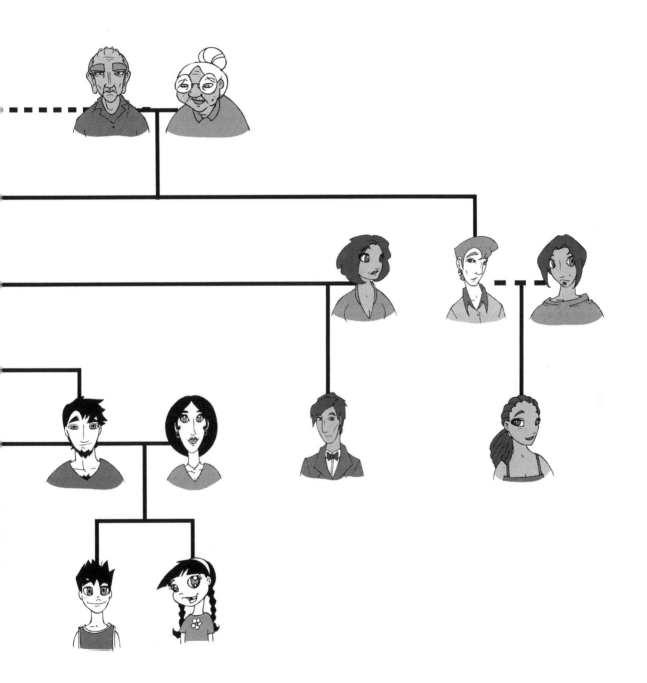

Exercise 1.12   The father of my father is my grandfather

Play the lineage game by filling in the blanks with the correct family terms. Don't get confused by the multiple levels of lineage. You might want to draw yourself some charts.

1.   El tata de mi vieja es mi _____.

2.   La hija de mi abue' es mi _____.

3.   La media naranja de mi padrastro es mi _____.

4.   El hijo de mi mami es mi _____.

5.   La 'mana de mi viejo es mi _____.

6.   La mami de mi hijo natural es mi _____.

7.   El 'mano del hijo de mi abue' es mi _____.

8.   La 'mana del hijo de mi tio es mi _____.

9.   El tata de mi primo es mi _____.

10. La abue' de mijo es mi _____.

Exercise 1.13   Talkin' with the fam

Respond with an appropriate greeting or response and a family term. For example, if the greeting says, "How's it going, Grandson?" You might respond, "Straight chillin', Gramps!"

1.   ¿Qué tal, tata?

_____

2.   ¿Cómo va todo, 'mana?

_____

3.   ¿Qué dices, mija?

_____

4.   ¿Qué haces, mi amante?

_____

5.   ¿Cómo andas, mi media naranja?

_____

Now create an appropriate greeting based on the response given.

6. _____

   Todo bien, mi viejo.

7. _____

   Ando ahí nomás, 'mano.

8. _____

   Todo tranqui', mijo natural.

9. _____

   Como siempre, madrastra.

10. _____

   Nada mucho, amante.

·····Describin' my peeps

Real talk. Let's be honest. Even your best friends get on your fuckin' nerves sometimes, right? It's important to be able to call them out at those moments as the fake, tacky assholes that they are. Use the terms below to describe all the new people you've learned about in this chapter and blow off some steam in the process. Spanish speakers are very warm, caring people. But they also talk mad shit. Knowing these terms will help you blend in.

SLANG BOX

ADJECTIVES		NOUNS	
Fake	Plástico	Buzzkill	Cortamambos
Tacky	Cursi	Party pooper	Aguafiestas
Trashy	Jarca	Wet blanket	Pinchaglobos
Bossy	Mandón/a	Party animal	Calavera
Pussy-whipped	Siquerida	Nerd	Nerdo
Boring	Pesado	Suck-up	Lambiscón/a
Lazy	Flojo	Ass-kisser	Lameculos

Exercise 1.14 True or false?

Think about whether the people in your life are being described accurately below. Then circle if the statement is true (verdadero) *or false* (falso).

1. Mi amigote es un nerdo pesado.   ***¿Verdadero o falso?***

2. Mi tata es un aguafiestas siquerida.   ***¿Verdadero o falso?***

3. Mi 'mano es un calavera flojo.   ***¿Verdadero o falso?***

4. Mi primo es un lambiscón cursi.   ***¿Verdadero o falso?***

5. Mi abue' es una cortamambos mandona.   ***¿Verdadero o falso?***

6. Mi amante es un/a lameculos siquerida.   ***¿Verdadero o falso?***

7. Mi media naranja es un/a pinchaglobos jarca.   ***¿Verdadero o falso?***

Exercise 1.15 Character Maps

Using the descriptions in the column on the left, put an x in each box that accurately describes the people from the rows at the top.

	Mi amigote	Mi tata	Mi abue'	Mi viejo	Mi amante	Mi 'mano/a	Mi media naranja
Flojo							
Siquerida							
Mandón/a							
Lameculos							
Nerdo							
Jarca							
Pinchaglobos							

Exercise 1.16 Who dat?

Use your newfound knowledge of people and descriptors to write out complete Spanish sentences describing the five examples pictured below. Try to use at least two new terms for each picture in your sentences. For example, if you see an old man staring with starstruck eyes at a woman leading him around on a dog leash, you might write (in Spanish): "That gramps is pussy-whipped!"

1. _____

_____

_____

_____

_____

2. _____

_____

_____

_____

_____

3. _____

_____

_____

_____

_____

4.

_____

_____

_____

_____

_____

5.

_____

_____

_____

_____

_____

Exercise 1.17   Friendly Mad Libs en español

Before reading the paragraph, fill in each blank with an appropriate term from the list below. Then translate the paragraph to see what hilarity you've unintentionally created.

Greetings	Good-byes	Family terms	Descriptive nouns	Descriptive adjectives
¿Qué tal?	Chao.	Tata	Cortamambos	Plástico
¿Qué pasa?	Me largo.	Mi viejo/a	Aguafiestas	Cursi
¿Qué haces?	Ahí nos vemos.	El/La abue'	Pinchaglobos	Jarca
¿Qué dices?		'Mano/a	Calavera	Mandón/a
¿Quihubo?	Nos huimos.	Hijo natural	Nerdo	Siquerida
¿Cómo va todo?	Hasta luego.	Primo/a	Lambiscón/a	Pesado
¿Cómo andas?		Tio/a	Lameculos	Flojo
		Padrastro/ Madrastra		
		Amante		
		Mijo/a		
		Mi media naranja		

Un día, mi (_____) me dice, "(_____)."
                (family term)   *(greeting)*

Yo respondo, "(_____), (_____)."
                        (greeting)   *(family term)*

Él/ella dice, "Tú eres un/a (_____) (_____)."
                                    (descriptive noun)   *(descriptive adjective)*

Yo respondo, "Gracias (_____). Tú eres el/la mejor (*the best*)
                              (family term)

(_____) y un/una (_____) (_____).
    (family term)   *(descriptive noun)*   *(descriptive adjective)*

(_____)." Él/ella dice, "(_____) (_____)
    (good-bye)   *(good-bye)*   *(descriptive noun)*

(_____)."
    (descriptive adjective)

Translate:

_____

_____

_____

_____

_____

_____

_____

CHAPTER 2

PARTY SPANISH
ESPAÑOL FIESTERO

Spanish speakers generally like to party their asses off. Whether it's a Mexican *quinciñera* or a dance club in Ibiza, Spanish speakers go hard. Hell, a night out on the town in Spain won't even begin until midnight, and you'll be lucky to be home by 7 a.m. So get your party lingo down cold if you want to bump it like they do in Barcelona or Buenos Aires.

·····Partyin'

There are a lot of different kinds of parties in the Spanish-speaking world, from a chilled-out backyard barbecue (*asado*) to an off-the-hook *reventón* that won't stop 'til day breaks.

SLANG BOX

NOUNS

House party	*Pachanga*	Megaparty	*Festejón*
Block party	*Festividad de barrio*	Blowout	*Reventón*
Club	*Club*	High-roller party	*Fiesta paquete*
Dance club	*Disco/Boliche*	Bachelor/ette party	*Despedida*
Dive	*Antro*	Titty bar	*Antro de vicio*
Rager	*Bacanal*	Whorehouse	*Ramería*

Exercise 2.1   Where's the party at?

Find and circle all of the party words below. Accents have been omitted.

Pachanga
Club
Boliche
Antro
Bacanal
Festejón
Reventón
Ramería

```
S   B   O   B   A   W   R   M   G   F   L

W   O   F   A   G   N   A   B   B   Y   C

I   L   E   C   A   U   M   Y   L   U   P

U   I   S   A   N   P   E   V   R   A   N

J   C   T   N   T   K   R   Q   C   O   C

N   H   E   A   R   Z   I   H   T   Z   L

I   E   J   L   O   I   A   N   T   N   U

H   F   O   Q   M   N   E   G   T   E   B

A   V   N   F   G   V   E   Q   R   A   K

H   Z   Q   A   E   G   S   R   B   X   Q

P   N   I   R   O   J   Y   V   H   N   K
```

Exercise 2.2   Label la fiesta

Match each party type below with the correct picture.

Festividad de barrio   _____

Club   _____

Antro   _____

Bacanal   _____

Fiesta paquete   _____

Despedida de soltera   _____

Antro de vicio   _____

d.

a.

e.

b.

f.

c.

g.

Exercise 2.3 Fill in the party!

Translate the party words in bold below to complete the sentences.

There are some hotties up in this house party!

Hay algunas bomboncitas en esta _____!

I'm gonna be smooth and hit on some sluts at the high-roller party!

Voy a ser suave y tirarse un lance a unas zorras a la _____!

Man, that shit was a megaparty!

Hombre, esa mierda era un _____!

Let's go to the dive bar first, hit up that rager, and end the night at the whorehouse!

Vamos al _____ primero, echar un vistazo a ese _____, y terminar la noche a la

_____!

For my bachelor party, I'm gonna have a blowout at the titty bar!

Para mi _____, voy a tener un _____ al _____!

·····Bumpin'

If a party is off the chain and you're getting crunk with your crew, you gots to let 'em know how fly that shit is. Here are a few phrases to show how you're straight chillin' when the party is bumpin'.

SLANG BOX

VERBS

To be bumpin'	*Estar a toda madre*	To get crunk	*Deschavetarse*
To get down	*Vacilar*	To dig	*Gozar*
To get your groove on	*Soltar una juerga*	To grind	*Hacer un perreo*

Exercise 2.4   Gettin' crunk with your gerunds

Sometimes a simple past tense statement just won't do. For instance, you would never say, "I ground all over that stripper's ass." You'd say, "I was grinding all over that stripper's ass." Luckily, there's a pretty simple way to do this in Spanish. You use a form of estar, estaba *(was), along with the gerund form of the verb you want (i.e., an "–ing" word: running, farting, fucking…).*

Step 1: Choose the right form of "was" (*estaba*).

I was	*Estaba*
You were	*Estabas*
He/She was	*Estaba*
We were	*Estabamos*
They were	*Estaban*

Step 2: Then, make your verb into an –**ing** ending.

-ar verbs end in "**ando**" (*nad**ando***)

-ir and -er verbs end in "-**iendo**" (*corr**iendo***; *sal**iendo***)

So, for example, "I was eating pussy" would be *Estaba comiendo la concha.* "You were eating pussy" would be *Estabas comiendo la concha.* Get it?

Now go practice conjugating the verbs below like in the examples above.

1. **To get down**   *Vacilar*

    I was gettin' down.   _____

    You were gettin' down.   _____

    He/She was gettin' down.   _____

    We were gettin' down.   _____

    They were gettin' down.   _____

2. **To get your groove on.**   *Soltar una juerga*

    I was gettin' my groove on.   _____

    You were gettin' your groove on.   _____

    He/She was gettin' his/her groove on.   _____

    We were gettin' our groove on.   _____

    They were gettin' their groove on.   _____

3. **To get crunk**   *Deschavetarse*

    I was gettin' crunk.   _____

    You were gettin' crunk.   _____

    He/She was gettin' crunk.   _____

    We were gettin' crunk.   _____

    They were gettin' crunk.   _____

4. **She was grindin' on my dick (*verga*).**   _____

5. **The club was bumpin'!**   _____

6. **I was gettin' crunk at the titty bar!**   _____

7. **You were diggin' that houseparty.**   _____

8. **I was grindin' on that ass (*culo*)!**   _____

Exercise 2.5   ¿Verdadero o falso?

That means true or false, gringo. Choose one.

1. Mujeres gozan cuando sus hombres vacilan al antro de vicio.   *¿Verdadero o falso?*

2. Hombres gozan cuando sus mujeres hacen un perreo con otros hombres en el club.   *¿Verdadero o falso?*

3. ¡La música de Kenny G está a toda madre!   *¿Verdadero o falso?*

4. Tú gozas deschavetarte a los antros más que los festejones.   *¿Verdadero o falso?*

5. Tu madre hace un perreo con muchos hombres a la ramería.   *¿Verdadero o falso?*

6. Prefieres vacilar a un estripclub de hombres.   *¿Verdadero o falso?*

7. ¡Los Amish tienen bacanales que están a toda madre!   *¿Verdadero o falso?*

8. Para el Año Nuevo vas a soltar una juerga con tres chicas a un reventón.   *¿Verdadero o falso?*

9. Tu despedida de soltero/a va a estar a toda madre a la ramería.   *¿Verdadero o falso?*

10. Te gusta deschavetarte con cocaína.   *¿Verdadero o falso?*

·····Drankin'

A party ain't a party until you get the drinks flowing. So start pouring and let the good times roll. Note that Spanish speakers like to drink, but unlike in the U.S., it's not considered cool to get so fucked up that you end up passed out in the bushes in front of the Sigma Chi house caked in your own vomit. You know who I'm talking about.

So if you want to make friends abroad, get your tolerance up and learn to pace yourself. Remember, the party might go all night, so five straight Jagerbombs at midnight might not be the best idea.

SLANG BOX

VERBS

To knock back a few	*Echar unas copas*	A drink	*Un trago*
To pound some shots	*Tragar algunos traguitos*	A bottle of beer	*Una botella de cerveza*
To get drunk	*Emborracharse*	A glass of wine	*Un vaso de vino*
To get crunk	*Deschavetarse*	A pint	*Una pinta*

NOUNS

A beer	*Una cerveza*
A brew	*Una birra*
A brewskie	*Una chela*
A shot	*Un traguito*

EXPRESSIONS

Cheers!	*¡Salud!*
Down the hatch!*	*¡Arriba, abajo, al centro, adentro!*

*Wherein the shot-takers put their drinks up, down, to the center and then they shoot.

Exercise 2.6   Reflexive partyin'

Some verbs in Spanish are reflexive, meaning that you tend to do them to yourself. For example, you don't just happen to become drunk, you get yourself drunk. You don't just get masturbated, you masturbate yourself. These verbs will generally have se *at the end of them (as in* masturbarse*). Depending on who you're referring to, that* se *will change to reflect the subject of the sentence. "I like to masturbate" is* Me gusta masturbarme. *"You like to masturbate" is* Te gusta masturbarte. *Follow the pattern below.*

Reflexive verb endings:

VERB FORM	REFLEXIVE VERB STEM
1st person (I/me/myself)	*Me*
2nd person (you/yourself)	*Te*
3rd person (he/she/himself/herself)	*Se*
1st person plural (we/us/ourselves)	*Nos*
3rd person plural (they/them/themselves)	*Se*

Fill in the correct reflexive verb stem then translate the sentences from Spanish to English.

1. Yo _____ emborracho cuando echo unas birras.

Translate: _____

2. Ella _____ deschaveta con los tragos en el club.

Translate: _____

3. Nosotros nos gusta emborrachar _____ cuando vacilamos a los bacanales.

Translate: _____

4. _____ emborrachas como una chiquita despues de dos chelas.

Translate: _____

5. Ellos estaban echando traguitos y deschavetando _____ al reventón.

Translate: _____

6. ¡Salud! ¡Vámonos a emborrachar _____!

Translate: _____

Exercise 2.7 Gettin' tipsy

Use the terms above to translate and complete the sentences below. Now go get crunk wit' it.

1. Let's get drunk and fuck!

    ¡Vámonos a _____ y coger!

2. Do you want to pound some shots from between my titties?

    ¿Quieres _____ de entre de mis chichis?

3. Let's knock back some brewskies and get crunk!

    ¡Vámonos a _____ y _____!

4. I got so drunk last night that I started taking shots out of some dude's butthole!

    ¡Me puse tan borracho anoche que comencé a tomar _____ del culo de algún tipo!

5. I want to get drunk on shitty beer and grind on some slutty bitches!

    ¡Quiero _____ con _____ de mierda y _____ con algunas perras zorras!

6. I need a stiff drink and a stiff dick!

   ¡Necesito un _____ fuerte y una polla dura!

7. Gimme a shot and a beer and get the fuck out of my way!

   ¡Dáme _____ y lárgate de mi puto camino!

8. To good friends, good beer, and good pussy. Cheers!

   A amigos buenos, _____ buena, y panocha buena. ¡_____!

SPECIALITY DRANKS

Mescal—The ugly stepsister of tequila, mescal will get you fucked up in a hurry and leave you with a splitting headache the morning after. It's essentially unrefined tequila, as it comes from the same agave plant that produces the Cuervos and Patrons of this world. You'll sometimes find a worm in the bottom of a bottle of mescal—hence the term "eat the worm."

Sangria—Sangria is a refreshing Spanish beverage made of sweet wine (usually red) and chopped up fruit. Sometimes brandy is added too, for an extra punch. On a hot summer day, nothing beats a glass of *sangria*.

Chicha—*Chicha* is corn liquor fermented by spit! Yep, old women in Peru will chew on some ground up maize, then spit it out and let it sit while the saliva breaks down the starch into sugar until it's ready to get you all liquored up. Delicious!

Michelada—You've heard of a Bloody Mary. Well, this is essentially a Bloody Beer. Parts beer, tomato juice, and lime juice, this red drink is often served in a salt-rimmed glass and with a bunch of spicy chile flakes tossed in. It's actually surprisingly delicious.

Aguardientes—The name means firewater, and it's just that. *Aguardientes* is the generic name for really strong hooch. In different countries, it's made from different things: fruit, corn, sugarcane. No matter what it's made from, it'll get you fucked up.

Exercise 2.8 Pick your poison

Use your newfound drinking knowledge to label each drink correctly (i.e., a glass of water, a pint of urine, etc.).

1. _____ 2. _____

3. _____ 4. _____

5. _____

•••••Drizunk!

Between tequila, *cerveza*, and sangria, a little drunkenness might happen every now and again. Embrace it!

SLANG BOX

ADJECTIVES

Sober	*Sobrio/a*	**Toasted**	*Cocido/a*
Buzzed	*Achispadito/a*	**Wasted**	*Fumigado/a*
Tipsy	*Choborra*	**Smashed**	*Picado/a*
Drunk	*Borracho/a*	**Fucked up**	*Hasta la mierda*

Exercise 2.9 Drunkeness quiz

Answer the questions below, then read on to see your drunkenness score.

A. Después de tres tragos, tú estás…

   1. sobrio.

   2. achispadito.

   3. picado.

B. Después de dos chelas, cuatro traguitos y una botella de vino, tú estás…

   1. choborra.

   2. hasta la mierda.

   3. muerto (dead).

C. Generalmente, no te gusta estar…

   1. sobrio.

   2. fumigado.

   3. borracho.

D. A las fiestas, te gusta estar…

   1. cocido.

   2. choborra.

   3. sobrio.

E. Todos los días, te pones (*you get*)…

    1. hasta la mierda.

    2. achispadito.

    3. ninguna de los anteriores (*none of the above*).

Add up all of your answers. For example, if for a, b, c, d, and e you answered 1, 3, 2, 2, 1, your total would be 9 (1+3+2+2+1).

If you scored:

5 points: *You're going to die from alcohol poisoning.*

6–8 points: *You're probably an alcoholic.*

9–12 points: *You enjoy partying but know your limits.*

13–15 points: *You need to lighten up and get a tolerance, you pussy.*

Exercise 2.10   True dat

*Choose true or false (*verdadero *or* falso*) for each of the statements about boozin' below.*

1. Sexo es mejor cuando estoy cocido.   ***¿Verdadero o falso?***

2. Prefiero ir a trabajo cuando estoy picado.   ***¿Verdadero o falso?***

3. Mi novio/a es más guapo/a cuando él/ella está fumigado.   ***¿Verdadero o falso?***

4. Yo soy más guapo cuando estoy hasta la mierda.   ***¿Verdadero o falso?***

5. Mis amigos son más interesantes cuando estoy sobrio.   ***¿Verdadero o falso?***

6. Chicas borrachas son más fáciles.   ***¿Verdadero o falso?***

7. Chicos picados son más inteligentes.   ***¿Verdadero o falso?***

8. Estar sobrio es aburrido.   ***¿Verdadero o falso?***

Exercise 2.11   You diggin' this house party?

Help this guy pick up his ladyfriend by translating the conversation below.

He said: _____   _____   _____

_____   _____   _____

She said: _____   _____   _____

_____   _____   _____

•••••The hangover

Though it's not cool to get completely wasted in most Spanish-speaking countries, let's be honest, it happens sometimes. Here are the terms you'll probably need to get through the morning after.

SLANG BOX

VERBS		To projectile vomit	*Lanzar*
To vomit	*Vomitar*	**To pass out**	*Desmayarse*
To puke	*Buitrear*	**To be hungover**	*Estar crudo*
To throw up	*Largar*	**To have a hangover**	*Tener un crudo*

Exercise 2.12   Like it? Or puke on it?

Respond to each question based on your own personal preferences. For questions 4–6, challenge yourself to write in complete sentences, you knuckle-dragger.

1.   ¿Te gustan los hipsters o quieres buitrearlos?

    a. Me gustan los hipsters.

    b. Quiero buitrearlos.

2.   ¿Te gustan los fratboys o quieres lanzarlos?

    a. Me gustan los fratboys.

    b. Quiero lanzarlos.

3.   ¿Te gusta Gandhi o quieres largarlo?

    a. Me gusta Gandhi.

    b. Quiero largarlo.

4.   ¿Te gustan chicas borrachas o quieres buitrearlas?

_____

5.   ¿Te gustan las tetas grandes o quieres lanzarlas?

_____

6.   ¿Te gusta el pene grande or quieres vomitarlo?

_____

Exercise 2.13   Alcohol tolerance check

Put an x in every column to show what happens when you have the number of drinks indicated. If you don't put any x's down, you have a problem, and it's called alcoholism.

Lo que pasa… (What happens…)	Número de tragos			
	Un trago	Tres tragos	Cinco traguitos	Diez chelas
Desmayarse				
Buitrear				
Hacer un perreo				
Tener un crudo				
Vacilar				
Estar hasta la mierda				

Exercise 2.14   The hangover doctor

Based on the "symptoms," choose the correct term being described.

1.   Cuando una persona traga muchos traguitos y duerme.

   a. Desmayarse

   b. Lanzar

   c. Tener un crudo

2.   Cuando una persona corra al bano para vomitar después de (*after*) su cuarto trago.

   a. Estar crudo

   b. Buitrear

   c. Vacilar

3.   Cuando un hombre baila con su pinga en las nalgas (*his dick on the booty*) de una mujer.

   a. Lanzar

   b. Desmayarse

   c. Hacer un perreo

4.   Cuando una persona está enferma la mañana después de muchas chelas.

   a. Estar crudo

   b. Largar

   c. Vacilar

5.   Cuando una persona vomita con mucha fuerza (*force/strength*).

   a. Lanzar

   b. Desmayarse

   c. Hacer un perreo

Exercise 2.15   Rico's big night out (and shitty morning after)

Rico had a big night last night. Unfortunately, he can't remember much. Help him put the pieces together by first labeling each picture with the correct partying terminology (i.e., drunk, hungover, projectile vomiting, etc). Then number the pictures in the order in which they presumably occurred. Finally, on the lines on page 39 write a short paragraph in Spanish describing Rico's big night.

A. _____

B. _____

C. _____

D. _____

E. _____

F. _____

G. _____

Correct Order	Write a short paragraph in Spanish describing Rico's night.
1. _____	_____
2. _____	_____
3. _____	_____
4. _____	_____
5. _____	_____
6. _____	_____
7. _____	_____
	_____

·····Druggin'

As you may have heard, a lot of drugs pass through Latin America on their way to our grateful American pipes, bongs, and needles. A lot of drugs are simple cognates of English words (*cocaína*, *heroína*, *marihuana*). Here are some of street names you might hear, though.

WEED

As in the U.S., weed is pretty popular in Mexico. Not surprising considering that Mexican food is just about the best munchies grub you could possibly imagine.

SLANG BOX

VERBS

To smoke	*Fumar*	A blunt	*Un porro*
To take a hit	*Tomar un toque*	A spliff	*Un canuto*
		A roach	*Un puchito bacha*
NOUNS		Pothead	*Fumero*
Weed	*La mota*		
Bud	*La marimba*	**ADJECTIVES**	
Herb	*La hierba*	High	*Drogado/a*
Hash	*La grifa*	Baked	*Cocido/a*
A joint	*Un pito*	Stoned	*Fumado/a*

Exercise 2.16   The sticky icky

Use your new drug words to answer the questions below correctly. Me pongo *means "I get" or "I become."*

1. Me pongo drogado en…

   a. chelas.

   b. agua.

   c. marimba.

2. Me pongo borracho en…

   a. mota.

   b. birra.

   c. hierba.

3. Fumo (*I smoke*)…

   a. los canutos.

   b. los traguitos.

   c. los tragos.

4. Un pito tiene… adentro (*inside*).

   a. la cerveza

   b. los canutos

   c. la mota

5. Marimba…

   a. me pone drogado/a.

   b. me pone borracho/a.

6. Chelas…

   a. me ponen drogado/a.

   b. me ponen borracho/a.

7. Me gusta fumar…

   a. la hierba.

   b. la verga.

   c. la chocha. (*pussy*)

8. La mota debe ser (*should be*)

   a. legal.

   b. ilegal.

Exercise 2.17 Searching for that high

Find the Spanish translation for each word below:

High

Weed

Bud

Herb

Hash

Joint

Spliff

Roach

Pothead

```
A  V  O  L  A  G  R  I  F  A
D  B  V  M  O  T  A  J  N  J
A  B  R  E  I  H  W  K  B  Y
F  B  L  F  U  M  E  R  O  L
W  B  M  O  D  A  G  O  R  D
H  P  V  I  W  W  Y  T  O  T
J  S  I  K  R  P  M  U  U  J
U  C  T  T  J  A  J  N  X  W
K  F  K  E  O  N  M  A  C  D
L  U  J  U  I  S  L  C  P  P
```

DOPE

Some people like to roll a little harder when they head out for a night on the town. And these are probably what they're rolling on.

SLANG BOX

NOUNS

Pills	*Pastis*	Roofies	*Burundungas*
Coke	*Perico*	Ecstasy	*Tacha*
Blow	*Nieve*	Cokehead	*Angurri*
Rock	*Piedra basuco*	Dope fiend	*Drograta*
Horse (heroin)	*El caballo jaco*	Junky	*Tecato/Falopero*

Exercise 2.18   Scrambled: This is your brain on drugs

Unscramble and translate the following drugs from Spanish to English:

1. eprioc _____ *Translation:* _____

2. udguarsnbun _____ *Translation:* _____

3. athac _____ *Translation:* _____

4. stapsi _____ *Translation:* _____

5. veine _____ *Translation:* _____

6. rbamiam _____ *Translation:* _____

7. aotm _____ *Translation:* _____

Exercise 2.19   Your best friend loves to get wasted on roofies because she's a cokehead.

Randomly choose six of your friends, six words that describe how fucked up someone is, six drugs, and six words to describe druggies. Plug them into the sentence equation to reveal all your friends' serious drug habits. Translate below.

DRUG VOCABULARY

TYPE OF HIGH	DRUG OF CHOICE	TYPE OF JUNKIE
achispadito/a	mota	un angurri
choborra/a	marimba	un drograta
borracho/a	pastis	un teco/falopero
cocido/a	perico	un fumero
fumigado/a	nieve	un addicto
picado/a	burundungas	
hasta la mierda	tacha	
drogado/a		
deschavetado/a		

Example:

Name of friend + *le encanta ponerse* + type of high + *en* + drug of choice + *porque es* + type of junkie.

     (loves to get)   *(on)*   *(because he/she is)*

Write six sentences following the example at left.

1. _____

Translation: _____

2. _____

Translation _____

3. _____

Translation: _____

4. _____

Translation: _____

5. _____

Translation: _____

6. _____

Translation: _____

Exercise 2.20   Drugs 101

It's important to know your drugs and their effects. If you don't, you might end up paying top dollar for some cheap-ass hash or a bag of baking powder you thought was coke. No one should have to suffer that pain. No one. Based on the effects described below, choose the correct drug being described. Te hace *means "makes you."*

1. Esta droga te hace tener hambre.

    a. Nieve

    b. Caballo jaco

    c. Mota

2. Esta droga te hace querer tener sexo.

    a. Marimba

    b. Tacha

    c. Piedra basuco

3. Esta droga te hace tener mucha energía.

    a. Perico

    b. Burundungas

    c. Mota

4.   Esta droga te hace desmayarte.

     a. Nieve

     b. Burundungas

     c. Tacha

5.   Esta droga te hace un falopero.

     a. Marimba

     b. Tacha

     c. Caballo jaco

6.   Un angurri quiere esta droga.

     a. Nieve

     b. Grifa

     c. Burundungas

Exercise 2.21   Bringing the whole party together

Let's see how much you learned this chapter. Create your own epic party sentences by combining words from each category below. If you can translate each one of your sentences without going back through the chapter, you're ready to party hard in Spanish.

PARTY VOCABULARY

TYPE OF HIGH	DRINK/DRUG	GETTING DOWN	PARTY PLACE
sobrio/a	birras	vacilando	pachanga
achispadito/a	chelas	soltando una juerga	club
choborro/a	traguitos	deschavetandome	disco/boliche
cocido/a	tragos	gozando	antro
fumigado/a	mota	haciendo un perreo	bacanal
picado/a	marimba	a toda madre	festejon
hasta la mierdo/a	hierba		reventon
drogado/a	pastis		fiesta paquete
deschavetado/a	perico		despedida solerto/a
	nieve		antro vicio
	piedra basuco		
	el caballo jaco		
	burundungas		
	tacha		

Example: ¡**Estaba** + <u>type of high</u> + **_en_** + <u>drink/drug</u> + **_y_** + <u>getting down</u> + **_al/a la_** + <u>party place</u>

(I am/ I was)   *(on)*   *(and)*   *(at the)*

1. _____

Translation: _____

2. _____

Translation: _____

3. _____

Translation: _____

4. _____

Translation: _____

5. _____

Translation: _____

BODY SPANISH
ESPAÑOL CORPORAL

Spanish is a very politically incorrect language. People call each other out based on their physical characteristics all the time. If you're fat, they'll call you Fatty. If you're black, they'll call you Blacky. Latinos just don't give a shit about being all proper. And Spanish speakers, like anybody else, love talking about each other's looks and bodies.

·····Sexy

If you're a woman in Latin America, you're gonna get cat-called. It's just how it works. It's a macho culture down there and men love to ogle women's bodies. But who can blame 'em? They're ain't nothing finer than a fine Latina. But have no fear, white girls. Latino dudes love blondes too.

SLANG BOX

ADJECTIVES		NOUNS	
Hot	*Bueno*	A hottie	*Una buenota*
Cute	*Lindo*	A cutie	*Una bomboncita*
Ripped	*Fornido*	A fox	*Un cuero*
Slim	*Delgado*		
Skinny	*Flaco*		
Sexy	*Rico*		

Exercise 3.1   Sexy true or false

1. Mi madre es una buenota.   *¿Verdadero o falso?*

2. Playboy Bunnies son cueros.   *¿Verdadero o falso?*

3. No me gusta el sexo con chicos/chicas delgados.   *¿Verdadero o falso?*

4. Yo soy fornido y rico.   *¿Verdadero o falso?*

5. Ser guapo y rico es más importante que ser inteligente.   *¿Verdadero o falso?*

Exercise 3.2   Sexy superlatives

Superlatives are extreme descriptions. For example, saying that someone is "the sexiest" or has "the biggest" ass are superlative statements. Anything that is the most—the biggest, the smallest, the best, the worst—is a superlative.

In Spanish, the word más *means "more." To say "the most" you would say* el más*. For example,* el culo más gordo *means "the most fat ass" or "the fattest ass." And if you want to get even more extreme with it you could say "the fattest ass in the world":* el culo más gordo del mundo. *Go ahead and fill in the blanks with people's names to create your own superlative sentences in Spanish.*

1. _____ es la chica más guapa de mi escuela/trabajo.

Translation: _____.

2. _____ es el hombre más fornido del mundo.

Translation: _____.

3. _____ es la persona más rica del mundo.

Translation: _____.

4. _____ es la persona más flaca del mundo.

Translation: _____.

5. _____ es la bomboncita con las tetas más grandes del mundo.

Translation: _____.

·····Fugly

Latinos come in all shapes and sizes, not all of them pretty. In fact, Mexico is now the second most obese country in the world after the good ol' US of A! We're still #1! USA! USA! USA!

SLANG BOX

ADJECTIVES		NOUNS	
Fugly	*Deforme*	Bignose	*Narigón/narigona*
Chubby	*Fofito/a*	Bigmouth	*Jetón/jetona*
Tubby	*Fofo/a*	Bigass	*Nalgón/culón/nalgona/culona*
Fatty	*Gordito/a*	Lardass	*Gordinflón/gordinflona*
		Beanpole	*Palancón/palanlona*

Exercise 3.3 Who you callin' fugly?

Check out each of the famous people below. Then write a sentence in Spanish describing each person, using your new vocabulary above. Try to use as many new vocab words as possible.

1. _____

_____

_____

2. _____

_____

_____

3. _____

_____

_____

4. _____

_____

_____

5. _____

_____

_____

Exercise 3.4   Fugly features

Using your knowledge of ugly people, choose the term that fits the sentence best.

1.   Una chica con una naríz grande es una _____.

   a. jetona

   b. narigona

   c. gordita

2.   Un hombre con una boca grande es un _____.

   a. feo

   b. nalgón

   c. jetón

3. Un chico gordo es un _____.

    a. gordinflón

    b. defeorme

    c. nalgón

4. Una chica con un culo grande es una _____.

    a. narigona

    b. palancona

    c. nalgona

5. Un niño flaco es un _____.

    a. fofo

    b. palancón

    c. gordito

Exercise 3.5 Fugly translations

Translate the bold word below to complete the Spanish sentences. Remember that in Spanish the adjective comes after the noun it's describing.

1. I love fucking **fugly lardasses**!

    ¡Me encanta coger _____ _____!

2. Your mom's a **chubby bigass**, but I'd still nail her.

    Tu madre es una _____ _____, pero todavía la clavaría.

3. Your sister is **a hottie**!

    ¡Tu hermana es _____!

4. Your brother is **ripped** and **sexy**!

    ¡Tu hermano es _____ y _____!

5. I like 'em **chubby**, **tubby**, and down to fuck.

    ¡Me les gustan _____, _____ , y con ganas de culear!

6. Sorry, I don't date **skinny**, broke **beanpoles**.

    Lo siento, pero no salgo con _____ y pobres.

Exercise 3.6   Label the pics

Check out the pics below, then label each one in Spanish accordingly. In other words, if you see someone with a fat ass below, call them a fatass in Spanish.

1. _____

2. _____

3. _____

4. _____

5. _____

6. _____

7. _____

8. _____

9. _____

·····Tits and ass

You can measure how much a culture values something by the number of words in the language that can be used to describe it. Eskimos are all about snow, which is why they supposedly have like a trillion words for snow in Eskimoish, or whatever the hell their language is called. And in English, we have about 1,000 words for titties. I think we have our priorities straight! Tits and ass are pretty damn important in Spanish too, so there's no shortage of terms used to describe them.

SLANG BOX

NOUNS

Breasts	*Senos*	Ass	*Culo*
Boobies	*Bubis*	Butt	*Cola*
Knockers	*Globos*	Butt cheeks	*Nalgas*
Titties	*Chichis*	Ass crack	*Raya del culo*
Tits	*Tetas*	Ass cheeks	*Ancas*
Nipples	*Pezones*	Big-booty ho	*Nalgona*
Chest	*Pecho*		

Exercise 3.7   Lick it or stick it?

Study the list of titty and ass words above. Then, without cheating by going back and looking at the translations, go through the following list and indicate whether you'd lick it (titties) or stick it (asses). After you've finished, go back and see how many titties you licked and asses you sticked. A perfect score will have you licking no asses and sticking no titties.

Lick it — Lamarlo   *Stick it* — Chingarlo

1. Globo   ***¿Lamarlo o chingarlo?***

2. Pezón   ***¿Lamarlo o chingarlo?***

3. Culo   ***¿Lamarlo o chingarlo?***

4. Tetas   ***¿Lamarlo o chingarlo?***

5. Ancas   ***¿Lamarlo o chingarlo?***

6. Trasero   ***¿Lamarlo o chingarlo?***

7. Chichi   ***¿Lamarlo o chingarlo?***

8. Raya del culo   ***¿Lamarlo o chingarlo?***

9. Nalga   ***¿Lamarlo o chingarlo?***

10. Bubis   ***¿Lamarlo o chingarlo?***

Exercise 3.8   Ass-backwards

Unscramble each Spanish titty or ass word below then translate it to English.

1. **seatt**   _____   *Translation:* _____

2. **uloc**   _____   *Translation:* _____

3. **oezpesn**   _____   *Translation:* _____

4. **rotsrae**   _____   *Translation:* _____

5. **iiccshh**   _____   *Translation:* _____

6. **sanac**   _____   *Translation:* _____

7. **bloogs**   _____   *Translation:* _____

8. **subbi**   _____   *Translation:* _____

9. **aglnano**   _____   *Translation:* _____

Exercise 3.9   That's a big-ass titty!

Choose the sentence that best describes the picture. You may need to know some of the following words to help you out.

WORD BANK

Saggy	Caído/a	Flabby	Flácido/a	Firm	Firme
Tiny	Chiquitito/a	Enormous	Enorme		

1.

   a. Nalgas grandes
   b. Chichis enormes
   c. Culo pequeño

2.

   a. Nalgas firmes
   b. Tetas chiquititas
   c. Culo flácido

3.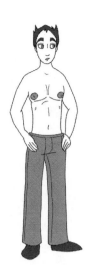

a. Pezones grandes

b. Ancas bonitas

c. Raya de culo pequeño

4.

a. Tetas flacas

b. Pezones firmes

c. Ancas flacas

Exercise 3.10   Find the nip

Find and circle the Spanish translations for each of the following T&A words:

Breasts

Knockers

Titties

Nipples

Ass

Butt

Butt cheeks

Ass cheeks

```
P  P  B  C  O  L  A  Z  X  U

G  S  U  Z  S  S  F  V  G  Y

Y  Z  B  F  P  O  Y  A  K  O

M  U  I  I  E  B  N  Y  A  J

O  J  S  O  Z  O  G  E  I  N

L  J  V  N  O  L  U  S  S  A

U  Q  O  G  N  G  G  M  L  L

C  I  B  M  E  E  G  H  H  G

Q  N  C  N  S  O  I  I  Q  A

C  H  I  C  H  I  S  U  A  S
```

Exercise 3.11   The biggest balls in the world!

Remember your superlatives from way back in the beginning of this chapter? Well, now that you've learned a few more dirty words you can make some way more badass superlatives. Go ahead and write a few sentences below about who has the biggest dick, the fattest asshole, and most giant pussy in the world. Get creative with it!

1. _____

2. _____

3. _____

4. _____

5. _____

DICK AND PUSSY

In the Horny chapter, you'll learn all of the words for dick and pussy. But here are a few of the essentials if you're a perv and can't wait that long:

Dick	*La verga*	**Pussy**	*La concha*
Balls	*Los huevos*	**Clit**	*La campana*

Exercise 3.12 *Limón*

There are lots of things that you can do to a lemon: squeeze it, pinch it, suck it, twist it. These also happen to be really fun things to do to genitals, titties, and asses. Without reading across the rows, fill in the chart below in Spanish. Then read across the rows or randomly mix-n-match to see which of your friends has been eating ass crack and who's been suckin' titty.

THINGS YOU CAN DO TO A LEMON

Lick	*Lama*	**Bite**	*Morde*
Grab	*Agarra*	**Eat**	*Come*
Pinch	*Pellizca*	**Squeeze**	*Exprime*
Twist	*Torce*	**Peel**	*Pela*
Suck	*Chupa*		

Muchachos The names of you and/or your 4 closest guy friends	*Limón* Things you can do to a lemon:	*Partes del cuerpo* 5 different sexual body parts	*Muchachas* The names of you and/or your 4 closest girl friends	*En/a lugares* 5 different paces

<u>Name of friend</u> + <u>thing you can do to a lemon</u> + <u>part of body</u> + <u>name of friend</u> + <u>places</u>

Write five sentences following the example above.

1. _____

2. _____

3. _____

4. _____

5. _____

·····Jelly bellies

After their sexual parts, people across the world are obsessed with their stomachs. It's no different in Spanish-speaking lands. There are terms to describe all types of tummies and bellies, from the firmest of the firm to the fattest of the fat. Here are some of the most colorful.

SLANG BOX

NOUNS

Belly	*Panza*	Rolls	*Rollos*
Spare tire	*Llanta*	Love handles	*Michelines*
Beer gut	*Guata*	Six-pack	*Tabla de chocolate*
Muffintop	*Bollito*	Washboard abs	*Tabla de lavar*

Exercise 3.13   Label that ass!

In Spanish, label the indicated body parts on each of the following drawings. Be as specific as possible.

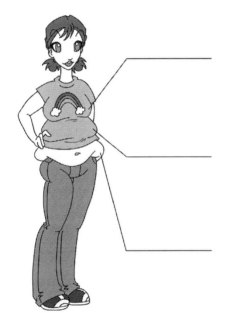

1.

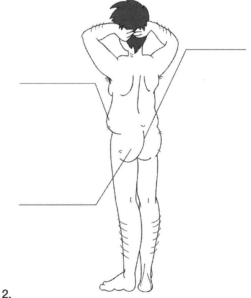

2.

3.   4.

Exercise 3.14   Dirty Pictionary

The word dibuja *means "draw." Follow the commands to draw the people being described. Don't forget to pay attention to the implied gender of the person.*

1. Dibuja una nalgona con globos grandes y una panza gorda.

2. Dibuja un jetón con pezones grandes, una llanta, y el rayo de culo visible.

3. Dibuja un gordinflona con un bollito, chichis enormes, y un culo gigante con muchos rollos.

4. Dibuja un cuero fornido y degado con una tabla de chocolate y dos ancas fuertes (*strong*).

Exercise 3.15   Who's got a fat ass?

Let's face it. Some of your friends and family are better looking than others. Put an x in every box that's an attribute of the person described in that column. You may need to refer back to the Friendly Spanish chapter to remember who some of these people are.

	Amigote	Amante	Tata	La abue'	Mi vieja	Hermano/a	El abue'
Chichis grandes							
Guata							
Nalgón/a							
Michelines							
Tabla de chocolate							
Un culo bueno							
Palancón							

·····Piss and shit

Latinos are obsessed with their own shit. In English, "fuck" is the strongest word. But in Spanish, because of their obsession with poop, "shit" is foulest of the foul. And with all the spicy food, mosquitoes, and nonpotable water you'll encounter in your travels, you'll have ample opportunity to employ this fine term.

For a few of the translations below, you may need to know how to use the phrases "have to" or "on myself." Follow the examples below.

I **have to** take a shit!   *¡Tengo que depositar un zurullo!*

I dropped a turd on **myself**!   *¡Me deposité un zurullo!*

SLANG BOX

VERBS

Drain the lizard	*Achicar la verga*
Hit the john	*Irme al trono*
To piss	*Mear*
To shit	*Cagar*
To take a shit	*Hacer una cagada*
To drop a turd	*Depositar un zurullo*
To have the shits	*Tener la cagadera*
To have diarrhea	*Tener una cursera*

NOUNS

Shit	*Mierda*
Diarrhea	*Cursera*

ADJECTIVE

Constipated	*Estreñido*

Exercise 3.16   Translate that shit!

Translate the shitty words in bold below to complete the Spanish sentences.

1. I have **diarrhea** from all that nasty **shit** your mom cooked.

    Tengo _____ de toda esa _____ asquerosa que tu madre cocinó.

2. I have **to shit** so bad but I'm **constipated** out the ass.

    Tengo que _____ tanto pero estoy _____ por el culo.

3. Baby, I'm going to **drop a turd** on your chest and fuck you in the **shit**.

    Nena, voy a _____ en tu pecho y chingarte en la _____.

4. Do you want **to piss** in my mouth and eat my **diarrhea**?

    ¿Quieres _____ en mi boca y comer mi _____?

5. I'm gonna **hit the john** and drain my big purple **lizard**.

    Voy a _____ y _____ grande y morada.

Exercise 3.17   Shitty translations

Conjugate the verbs below in the present and past tense, using the following examples to guide you. Then translate the sample sentences using vocabulary you already know.

Example:

To drop a turd	*Depositar un zurullo*	**I dropped a turd**	*Deposité un zurullo*
I drop a turd	*Deposito un zurullo*	**You dropped a turd**	*Depositaste un zurullo*
You drop a turd	*Depositas un zurullo*	**He/She dropped a turd**	*Depositó un zurullo*
He/She drops a turd	*Deposita un zurullo*	**We dropped a turd**	*Depositamos un zurullo*
We drop a turd	*Depositamos un zurullo*	**They dropped a turd**	*Depositaron un zurullo*
They drop a turd	*Depositan un zurullo*		

A.   To shit   *Cagar*

I shit _____   I shat _____

You shit _____   You shat _____

He/She shits _____   He/She shat _____

We shit _____   We shat _____

They shit _____   They shat _____

I have to take a shit! _____

I shat my pants! _____

She shat a giant turd! _____

My girlfriend ate Indian food and shat the bed! _____

_____

B. To piss   *Mear*

I piss _____   I pissed _____

You piss _____   You pissed _____

He/She pisses_____   He/She pissed _____

We piss _____   We pissed _____

They piss _____   They pissed _____

I have to take a piss! _____

I pissed myself! _____

You pissed the bed! _____

CHAPTER 4

HORNY SPANISH
ESPAÑOL CALIENTE

Nothing turns on a fine piece of ass like a hot Spanish accent (though you may want to avoid the Castilian lisp—that's pretty gay). And if you can actually speak a few dirty sex words in Spanish while faking your accent, so much the better. You'll soon be knee-deep in pussy (or testicles, if that's your thing). Now if you're like most people using this workbook, you probably skipped right to this chapter. But don't get your rocks off just yet. These lessons build on each other and nobody likes a lover who doesn't take their time. Except for men; men love that shit. So go slow and deep and make sure you really absorb all this dirty, dirty sexual knowledge.

•••••Fucking

Like in English, there are lots of different ways to say "let's fuck" in Spanish, from the romantic "let's make love" to the slightly more vivid "I wanna nail that ass."

SLANG BOX

VERBS

To fuck	*Coger*	To hook up	*Ligar*
To screw	*Culear*	To leave it raw	*Fregarla*
To bone	*Joder*	To have a quickie	*Echar un rapidín*
To hit that	*Comérsela*	To get your rocks off	*Echar un polvo*
To nail that ass	*Clavar ese culo*	To buttfuck	*Encular*
To make love	*Hacer el amor*		

Exercise 4.1   Fucking conjugations

If you've ever taken a Spanish class, you probably remember pointlessly conjugating a bunch of boring-ass verbs that you didn't give a shit about then and can't remember now. That's 'cause conjugating is boring as hell. Who cares how to say, "I swim, you swim, we swim"? If only your teachers had taught you a few words you actually gave a rat's ass about, you might still remember what the hell the pluperfect past tense subjunctive case is. Here are a few words that might come more in handy in life. Just remember that most "I" verbs end in "o." "You" verbs end in "s." "He/She" verbs end in "a" or "e." "We" verbs end in "mos," and "they" verbs end in "n." For example:

To eat pussy	*Comer la concha*
I eat pussy	*Yo como la concha*
You eat pussy	*Tú comes la concha*
He/She eats pussy	*Él/Ella come la concha*
We eat pussy	*Nosotros comemos la concha*
They eat pussy	*Ellos comen la concha*

Now it's your turn! See if you can conjugate the highly useful verbs below. Then try to use them correctly in the example sentences given.

A.   To buttfuck   *Encular*

1. I buttfuck   _____

2. You buttfuck   _____

3. He/She buttfucks   _____

4. We buttfuck   _____

5. They buttfuck   _____

6. I'm going to buttfuck your mom tonight.

   Voy a _____ a tu madre esta noche.

7. Our neighbors buttfuck like gay rabbits.

   Nuestros vecinos _____ como conejos mariposas.

8. Catholic girls buttfuck like crazy so they can stay "virgins."

   Chicas católicas _____ como locas para permanecer "vírgenes."

B. To fuck   *Coger*

1. I fuck   _____

2. You fuck   _____

3. He/She fucks   _____

4. We fuck   _____

5. They fuck   _____

6. I fuck fags for fun.

   Yo _____ mariposas para divertirme.

7. You fuck like a slut.

   Tú _____ como una zorra.

8. She only fucks in the ass.

   Ella solo _____ en el culo.

C. To screw   *Culear*

1. I screw   _____

2. You screw   _____

3. He/She screws   _____

4. We screw   _____

4. They screw   _____

5. We screw all night! _____

   ¡Nosotros _____ toda la noche!

7. I want to screw you in the mouth.

   Quiero _____ te en la boca.

8. He only screws without condoms.

   Él solo _____ sin condones.

D. **To bone**   *Joder*

   1. I bone   _____

   2. You bone   _____

   3. He/She bones   _____

   4. We bone   _____

   5. They bone   _____

   6. Men make love. Boys bone.

      Hombres hacen el amor. Niños _____.

   7. I bone bitches like I don't give a fuck.

      Yo _____ perras como no me importa una mierda.

   8. She loves to bone!

      ¡A ella le encanta _____!

Exercise 4.2   I will bone you here and there, I will bone you everywhere!

Use the pictures to help you translate the phrases in bold below and you'll learn some good places to make sex!

1. *A ella le encanta joder en **el coche**.*

    She loves to bone in _____.

2. *A ella le encanta joder en **la ducha**.*

    She loves to bone in _____.

3. *A ella le encanta joder en **la cama**.*

    She loves to bone in the _____.

4. *A ella le encanta joder en **el piso**.*

    She loves to bone on _____.

5. *A ella le encanta joder en* **la piscina**.

    She loves to bone in _____.

EXERCISE 4.3 WHO FUCKS WHO?

Choose the best answer that completes the sentence.

1. **Han Solo liga con _____.**

    a. Luke Skywalker   b. Darth Vader   c. Princess Leia   d. Chewbacca

2. **Marge Simpson _____ con Lisa.**

    a. culea   b. coge   c. habla   d. clava ese culo

3. **Barack Obama le gusta fregarla con _____.**

    a. Hillary Clinton   b. Jill Biden   c. Monica Lewinsky   d. Michelle Obama

4. **Papa Smurf echa un polvo con _____.**

    a. Gargamel   b. Smurfette   c. Mama Smurf   d. todos los smurfs

5. **Marilyn Monroe culea con _____.**

    a. JFK   b. Joe DiMaggio   c. Marlon Brando   d. todos los anterior (*all of the above*)

Exercise 4.4 Best fucking guess

Respond to the questions in complete sentences. The answers should be obvious, so concentrate on writing the fucking words right.

1. ¿Santa Claus culea con quién?

_____

2. ¿Tu madre echa rapidines con quién?

_____

3. ¿Snow White coge con quién?

_____

4. ¿Con quién liga Aladdin?

_____

5. ¿A quién tú quieres joder?

_____

Exercise 4.5 Sex commands

Sometimes you gotta tell your partner what you want in the bedroom, especially if you're a girl. If you don't, your guy is just gonna zero in on that pussy with his red rocket, give it a few pumps and roll over and go to bed. For some reason, girls don't like that. So tell your Latin lover what you want by using these aggressive sexual commands. Suck me, bitch!

To make a verb a command, just say it in the third person, but more aggressively. So for example, chupar *means "to suck." The phrase* chupa la verga *means "he/she sucks cock" but it's also the command "suck the cock!" The difference is all in the delivery.*

If you wanted to say "Suck me!" you would say chúpame *with the accent on the first syllable. "Suck it!" would be* chúpalo.

SLANG BOX

VERBS

To lick	*Lamar*	To stroke	*Acariciar*
To suck	*Chupar*	To shave	*Afeitar*
To eat	*Comer*	To cum	*Lechear*
To rub	*Frotar*	To hit	*Pegar*
To touch	*Tocar*	To manhandle	*Manotear*
To grab	*Agarrar*		

Translate the words or phrases below.

1. Eat me!

   ¡_____!

2. Lick me!

   ¡_____!

3. Stroke my balls!

   ¡_____ mis huevos!

4. Manhandle my pussy!

   ¡_____ mi concha!

5. Grab my tits and cum on my face!

   ¡_____ mis tetas y _____ en mi cara!

·····Dick and pussy

Wanna whip out your cock and dip your nuts in the cooch 'til you get a boner with a shaft hard enough to rub on the clit while you fingerbang the poontang? There are a plethora of terms in Spanish to refer to everyone's favorite organs.

SLANG BOX

NOUNS

Nuts	Las bolas	Pussy	La concha
Balls	Los huevos	Clam	La almeja
Penis	El pene	Carpet	La alfombrita
Boner	La puntada	Cooch	La chucha
Dick	El pito	Poontang	La chocha
Cock	La verga	Cunt	El coño
Shaft	La pinga	Cameltoe	El hachazo
Head	La cabeza	Clit	La campana
Little dick	El cacahuate	Lips	Las labias

Exercise 4.6   Cock search

Circle all the dick and pussy words in Spanish below.

Bolas

Campana

Chucha

Coño

Huevos

Puntada

Verga

N	N	Z	A	C	H	U	C	H	A
H	J	T	Z	H	U	E	V	O	S
K	I	K	J	H	U	M	F	E	P
G	T	A	H	C	N	O	C	W	U
Y	E	Z	M	A	B	S	C	T	N
V	D	A	L	M	B	F	O	Q	T
D	E	A	Z	P	O	B	Ñ	V	A
F	Z	R	W	A	L	B	O	W	D
W	U	N	G	N	A	O	W	R	A
E	L	Q	V	A	S	V	A	K	M

Exercise 4.7 Dick pics and muff shots

In the boxes provided below, draw the male and female members labeling them with vocabulary from the slang box on page 70.

El Pito

La Concha

Exercise 4.8 Scrambled pussy

Unscramble the genital words below and write the translation on the line next to it.

1. hchcao _____   *Translation:* _____

2. ovuhes _____   *Translation:* _____

3. greva _____   *Translation:* _____

4. hcncao _____   *Translation:* _____

5. dpnuata _____   *Translation:* _____

6. pcnmnaaa _____   *Translation:* _____

Exercise 4.9   Two dicks are better than one

In English, we don't have a plural form for possessive pronouns (my, your, his, etc.). You use the same form as in the singular. For example, if you have one testicle you'd say "my ball." If you have two testicles, you'd say "my balls." The "my" doesn't change. Not the case in Spanish, however. One teste *would be* "mi huevo." *Two nuts would be* "mis huevos." *Notice how the* mi *changes to* mis?

	Singular	Plural
My	*Mi*	*Mis*
Your	*Tu*	*Tus*
His/Her	*Su*	*Sus*
Our	*Nuestro/a*	*Nuestros/as*
Their	*Su*	*Sus*

Choose the correct translation.

1. My nuts hurt.
   a. *Me duelen mis pitos.*
   b. *Me duele mi bola.*
   c. *Me duelen mis bolas.*
   d. *Me duele mi coño.*

2. Your pussy smells like shit!
   a. *¡Tu verga huele de mierda!*
   b. *¡Tu concha huele de mierda!*
   c. *¡Tus chuchas huelen de mierda!*
   d. *¡Tus huevos huelen de mierda!*

3. Their dicks are tiny.
   a. *Sus pitos son pequeños.*
   b. *Su pito es pequeño.*
   c. *Sus hachazos son pequeños.*
   d. *Su puntada es pequeña.*

4. Put your balls on my clit.
   a. *Pon tus huevos en mis campanas.*
   b. *Pon tu huevo en mi campana.*
   c. *Pon tu huevos en mis campanas.*
   d. *Pon tus huevos en mi campana.*

5. Our cocks like to touch.
   a. *Nuestras vergas les gusta tocar.*
   b. *Nuestra verga le gusta tocar.*
   c. *Nuestras pingas les gusta tocar.*
   d. *Nuestra pinga le gusta tocar.*

Translate your own:

6. I like your pussy. _____

7. My balls are big. _____

8. Do you want my dick in your poontang? _____

9. My cock is bigger than their cocks. _____

10. Rub your shaft on my clit. _____

·····Dirty Talk

Dressing up like a Furry and dripping hot wax on your boyfriend's taint isn't for everyone. But who among us doesn't like a little dirty talk every now and then?

Exercise 4.10 Talkin' dirty

Make your own dirty sentences by combining one word from each box below. But don't forget to conjugate each verb first by writing it in the command form (remember: same as the third person).

Also remember that in Spanish, adjectives always come after the nouns. So "dirty pussy" is concha sucia *not* sucia concha. *And the adjective always reflects the gender and quantity of the noun it's describing.*

Singular masculine: *El pito pequeño* (The little dick)   **Plural masculine:** *Los pitos pequeños* (The little dicks)

Singular feminine: *La teta gorda* (The fat tit)   **Plural feminine:** *Las tetas gordas* (The fat tits)

Sexual Commands/Verbs	Connectors	Body Parts	Adjectives
To lick *Lamar*	**My** *Mi/Mis*	**Pussy** *Concha*	**Big** *Grande*
To eat *Comer*	**Your** *Tu/Tus*	**Cunt** *Coño*	**Small** *Pequeño*
To rub *Frotar*	**Me** *Me*	**Clit** *Campana*	**Dirty** *Sucio*
To touch *Tocar*	**With** *Con*	**Cock** *Verga*	**Fat** *Gordo*
To grab *Agarrar*	**In** *En*	**Dick** *Pito*	**Smelly** *Pudrido*
To play with *Jugar con*	**On** *En*	**Shaft** *Pinga*	**Wet** *Mojado*
To put *Poner*	**And** *Y*	**Balls** *Huevos*	**Giant** *Gigante*
To put in *Meter*		**Nuts** *Bolas*	**Sweaty** *Sudadoso*
To stroke *Acariciar*		**Tits** *Tetas*	**Hard** *Duro*
To manhandle *Manotear*		**Titties** *Chichis*	**Hot** *Caliente*
To shave *Afeitar*		**Nipples** *Pezones*	
To hit *Pegar*		**Mouth** *Boca*	
To cum *Lechear*		**Face** *Cara*	
To take *Tomar*		**Hand** *Mano*	
To take out *Sacar*		**Ass** *Culo*	
To fuck *Coger*		**Tongue** *Lengua*	
To screw *Culear*		**Finger** *Dedo*	
To suck *Chupar*			

Example:

(Sexual Command) + (Connector) + (Body Part) + (Adjective)

Lama + mi + concha +mojada = *Lick my wet pussy.*

Sexual Command	Connector	Body Part	Adjective

1. _____   _____   _____   _____

Translation: _____

2. _____   _____   _____   _____

Translation: _____

3. _____   _____   _____   _____

Translation: _____

4. _____

Translation: _____

5. _____   _____   _____   _____

Translation: _____

Translate:

6. *Lick my hot pussy with your wet tongue.*

_____

7. *Put my hard dick in your dirty cunt.*

_____

8. *Rub my sweaty nipples with your giant balls.*

_____

9. *Stroke me with your fat cock.*

_____

10. *Manhandle my smelly pussy!*

_____

Exercise 4.11   I gargle my sister's smelly balls

Fill in the chart below. Then read across the lines or mix and match to reveal your friends' hilarious sexual perversions. You might find that your best friend manhandled your sister's big shaft at your mom's house. Use the list from the previous exercise if you need help filling out the chart.

People	Sex Verb (3rd person)	Body Part (Sexual)	Adjective	of	People	a/in	Place
Mi amigote (My best friend)	*manotea*	*la pinga*	*grande*	*de*	*mi hermana* (my sister)	*a/en*	*la casa de tu mama*
(You)				*de*	(Friend 6)	*a/en*	
(Friend 1)				*de*	(Friend 7)	*a/en*	
(Friend 2)				*de*	(Friend 8)	*a/en*	
(Friend 3)				*de*	(Friend 9)	*a/en*	
(Friend 4)				*de*	(Friend 10)	*a/en*	

·····Blow jobs, circle jerks, etc.

Vaginal play lost its luster? Tired of good ol' penetration? Well *bienvenido a América Latina!* Latinas are really fucking good at noncoital sextras like BJ's and shit because they're all Catholics and aren't supposed to fuck until marriage. But nobody said anything about not eatin' pussy or givin' rim jobs and snowballs.

SLANG BOX

NOUNS

A blow job	*Una mamada*	Cunnilingus	*El buceo*
A hand job	*La paja*	A snowball	*Un beso blanco*
Dry humping	*La frottage*	A rim job	*El beso negro*
A circle jerk	*Una carrera de pajas*	A golden shower	*La lluvia dorada*
A circle suck	*Una margarita*	69	*Sesenta y nueve*
Some backdoor action	*La trastienda*		

Exercise 4.12   True or false

1. Hugh Grant recibe mamadas de prostitutas.   *¿Verdadero o falso?*

2. The Easter Bunny le gusta hacer la frottage con the Tooth Fairy.   *¿Verdadero o falso?*

3. Dick Cheney le da besos negros a Nancy Pelosi.   *¿Verdadero o falso?*

4. Frodo quiere la trastienda de Sam.   *¿Verdadero o falso?*

5. Hermione le gusta cuando Ron le hace el buceo y Harry mira.   *¿Verdadero o falso?*

6. R. Kelly da las lluvias doradas a los niños.   *¿Verdadero o falso?*

7. La frottage es mejor que (*is better than*) la sesenta y nueve.   *¿Verdadero o falso?*

8. Una paja es mejor que una mamada.   *¿Verdadero o falso?*

9. Elton John le gusta la trastienda.   *¿Verdadero o falso?*

10. Los Slytherin les gusta hacer la carrera de pajas con Voldemort.   *¿Verdadero o falso?*

Exercise 4.13   What the fuck is a snowball?

Don't feel bad if you don't know what a snowball, rim job, golden shower, or circle jerk is. In fact, you're probably a better person if you don't know those things. But for those of you who think you're pretty sexually savvy, see if you can identify each of the following sextras.

1. Una mamada es cuando una persona…
   a. *chupa la verga.*
   b. *juega con la campana.*
   c. *come la almeja.*
   d. *toca el coño.*

2. Un beso blanco es cuando una persona…
   a. *le da una mamada y escupe el semen en la boca del otro.*
   b. *lama el culo.*
   c. *le da una mamada mientras* (while) *el otro hace el buceo.*
   d. *chupa la campana.*

3. Sesenta y nueve es cuando una persona…
   a. *chupa la verga.*
   b. *lama el culo.*
   c. *chupa la verga mientras la otra persona hace el buceo.*
   d. *juega con la campana.*

4. Un beso negro es cuando una persona…

    a. *juega con la campana.*

    b. *masturba en un círculo.*

    c. *come la almeja.*

    d. *lama el culo.*

5. Una carrera de pajas es cuando muchas personas…

    a. *laman el culo.*

    b. *masturban en un círculo.*

    c. *comen semen.*

    d. *juegan con el coño.*

·····Sex Positions

Like with foods and colors, everyone has a favorite sex position. And some—like the color blue, pepperoni pizza, and doggy-style sex—are just objectively better than others. Some people—the very religious mostly—will insist that missionary is the best. Wrongheaded as it may seem, we must allow them their poor taste, lest we become a dictatorial state where women cover their beauty with burkas and men honor kill their daughters for having sex before marriage. Because if I had to choose between being Mormon or being Iranian, I'd choose Mormon every goddamn time. Hello, missionary sex!

SLANG BOX

NOUNS

Missionary	*El misionero*	**Spoon**	*En cuchara*
Doggy-style	*Perrito*	**Legs up**	*El candelabro*
Cowgirl	*Cabalgando*	**Reverse cowgirl**	*Cabalgando hacia atrás*
Wheelbarrow	*La gran carretilla*		

Exercise 4.14   Draw that position!

Draw the following positions in the boxes provided:

1. Perrito

2. Cabalgando hacia atrás

3. La gran carretilla

4. El misionero

5. El candelabro

6. En cuchara

PREPOSITIONS

Encima de	*On top of*	**Detrás de**	*Behind*
Debajo de	*Underneath*	**El hombre**	*The man*
En frente de	*In front of*	**La mujer**	*The woman*

Exercise 4.15A   Know your positions

In the heat of the moment, you might not always refer to your desired sex position by name because, let's face it, some of them sound pretty crass. Instead of blurting out, "I wanna fuck you cowgirl style!" you might just say, "Get on top of me." So it's important to know your directional words in Spanish.

1. En el misionero, el hombre está…

    a. *detrás de la mujer.*

    b. *encima de la mujer.*

    c. *en frente de la mujer.*

    d. *debajo de la mujer.*

2. En el perrito, el hombre está…

    a. *detrás de la mujer.*

    b. *encima de la mujer.*

    c. *en frente de la mujer.*

    d. *debajo de la mujer.*

3. En cabalgando, la mujer está…

    a. *detrás del hombre.*

    b. *encima del hombre.*

    c. *en frente del hombre.*

    d. *debajo del hombre.*

4. En mi posición favorita, yo estoy…

    a. *detrás de la mujer/el hombre.*

    b. *encima de la mujer/el hombre.*

    c. *en frente de la mujer/el hombre.*

    d. *debajo de la mujer/el hombre.*

5. En mi posición favorita, mi pareja (*partner*) está…

    a. *detrás de mi.*

    b. *encima de mi.*

    c. *en frente de mi.*

    d. *debajo de mi.*

Exercise 4.15B   Know your body

Complete the sentences below based on the pictures by using your new direction words.

1. La mujer está _____ del hombre.

2. El hombre está _____ de la mujer.

3. La mujer está _____ del hombre.

4. La mujer está _____ del hombre.

Exercise 4.16 What's your favorite po-zish?

Answer the following questions with the best possible answer.

1. Scooby Doo prefiere....

    a. el misionero.

    b. el perrito.

    c. cabalgando.

    d. en cuchara.

2. Bob the Builder prefiere…

    a. el misionero.

    b. el perrito.

    c. la gran carretilla.

    d. en cuchara.

3. Pope John Paul prefiere…

    a. el misionero.

    b. el perrito.

    c. la gran carretilla.

    d. en cuchara.

4. John Wayne prefiere…

    a. el misionero.

    b. el perrito.

    c. cabalgando.

    d. en cuchara.

·····Booty calls and fuck buddies

For better or worse, we typecast people based on their sexual habits in relation to us. So it's important to have the appropriate vocabulary to be able to separate your sluts from your whores and your fuck buddies from your friends with benefits.

SLANG BOX

A husband/wife	*Un/a esposo/a*	A fuck buddy	*Un/a tragón/a*
A boyfriend/girlfriend	*Un/a novio/a*	A lover	*Un/a amante*
A couple	*Una pareja*	A womanizer/player	*Un/a mujeriego*
A hookup	*Una liga*	A slut	*Un/a zorra*
A friend with benefits	*Un/a amigovio/a*	A whore	*Un/a puta*
A booty call	*Un/a consuelo sexual*	A prostitute	*Un/a prostituta*
		A virgin	*Un/a virgen*

Exercise 4.17   The perfect lover

Match one celebrity from the list to each phrase to determine who would be your lover, who would be your whore, who would be your spouse, etc. You can only use each celebrity once, however. So choose wisely.

1. Mi amigovio/a
2. Mi tragón/a
3. Mi esposo/a
4. Mi puta
5. Mi amante
6. Mi liga
7. Mi consuelo sexual
8. Mi novio/a

a. Jessica Rabbit
b. Mother Teresa
c. Smurfette
d. Oprah
e. Marilyn Monroe
f. Wonder Woman
g. Queen Latifah
h. Beyonce
i. Jesus
j. George Bush
k. Gandhi
l. Bill Cosby
m. Arnold Schwarzenegger
n. Santa Claus
o. Chuck Norris
p. Sean Connery

Exercise 4.18   Marry, fuck, kill

From the groupings below, choose who you would marry (casar), who you would fuck (coger), and who you would kill (matar).

1. Simba	Scar	Pumba
_____	_____	_____
2. Jasmine	Aladdin	The Genie
_____	_____	_____
3. George Washington	George Bush	George Clooney
_____	_____	_____
4. Belle	Ariel	Pocahontas
_____	_____	_____
5. Hillary Clinton	Chelsea Clinton	Monica Lewinsky
_____	_____	_____

Exercise 4.19   Girlfriend or slut?

Determine the sexual relationship based on the clues below.

1. Marissa es mi amiga y tenemos sexo. Ella es mi _____.

2. Tomás es mi novio. Somos una _____.

3. Cuando quiero culear, llamo a Diego porque él es mi _____.

4. Cuando tengo sexo con una persona y no hablo con él/ella otra vez, es una _____.

5. Yo pago Maria para sexo porque ella es una _____.

6. Ricardo es mi esposo pero culeo a Alejandro porque él es mi _____.

7. Elisa nunca tiene sexo. Ella es una _____.

8. Eduardo y Mariel tienen sexo con muchas personas. Él es un _____ y ella es una

    _____.

Exercise 4.20   What would you do?

Hypothetical situation: You really want to fuck in the ass. But you're afraid that if you fucked your partner in the ass, you would no longer respect them. So what do you do? Go for it? Hold off? Fuck a prostitute in the ass instead? Or maybe that hottie down the hall? If he/she wasn't your wife or husband, but simply a relationship or even a random hookup, would you do it? I guess what I'm trying to say is that the things you do in bed sometimes depend on who you're doing them with.

Now let's figure out where you stand on these important moral-sexual questions. Put an x in any box to indicate that you would perform the sextra from that column with the person named in that row.

	Sextras						
	Mamada	Perrito	La gran caretilla	La trastienda	El buceo	El beso negro	Sesenta y nueve
Esposo/a							
Novio/a							
Amigovio/a							
Consuelo sexual							
Puta							
Una liga							
Zorra/mujeriego							
Virgen							

Exercise 4.21   Grammar: *Un prostituta* or *una prostituta*?

Articles ("the" and "a") are tricky in Spanish. They change depending on the gender and number of objects being discussed. You use el, los, un, *and* unos *for masculine words, and* la, las, una, *and* unas *for feminine words. So if there are a bunch of dead prostitutes in your trunk, you'd say* unas prositutas muertas. *But if there's just one dead prostitute, it's* una prostituta muerta. *And if your dead hooker has a schlong he'd be* un prostituta muerto. *Get it?*

Read the dialogue and fill in the blanks with either un *or* una. *Use the slang bank to help you with any words you don't know. All other slang in the dialogue has been taught elsewhere in this chapter.*

SLANG BANK

Caliente	*Horny*	**Mariposa**	*Faggot*
Cállate	*Shut up*	**El consolador**	*Dildo*

Emilio: Estoy caliente. Quiero coger _____ puta con _____ conosolador grande y negro.

Juan: ¿Tienes _____ consolador?

Emilio: No. Está en la casa de _____ ex-novia.

Juan: Es _____ problema. Es difícil coger _____ puta sin _____ consolador.

Emilio: Yo sé. ¿Qué quieres hacer?

Juan: Quiero mamar _____ teta.

Emilio: Cállate. Eres _____ mariposa. Solo quieres mamar _____ pinga.

Exercise 4.22 Sexessories

Sometimes a good hard cock isn't enough to get the job done. That's why God invented the vibrator. Try to memorize the slang box below, then match the Spanish word for the sex toy/accessory with its picture.

SLANG BOX

NOUNS

A rubber	*Un impermeable / Un forro*	A gag	*Una mordaza*
		A blindfold	*Una venda*
A dildo	*Un consolador*	A paddle	*Una paleta*
A vibrator	*Un vibrador*	Handcuffs	*Esposas*
A tickling cock ring	*Un párpado de cabra*		

1. Una paleta _____

a.

2. Un vibrador _____

b.

3. Esposas _____

c.

4. Un párpado de cabra _____

d.

5. Un impermeable _____

e.

6. Una mordaza _____

f.

7. Un consolador _____

g.

8. Una venda _____

h.

Exercise 4.23   Sexual Mad Libs

The following sexual Mad Lib is going to put all your Horny Spanish knowledge to the test. First, decide who Person 1 and Person 2 will be (they can be you and your friends or famous people; doesn't really matter). Then fill in all the blanks to create your own sexual Mad Lib. Use the chart below with all the new words you've learned in this chapter to help you out.

FUCK WORDS

Coger
Culear
Joder
Comersela
Clavar ese culo
Hacer el amor
Ligar
Fregarla
Echar un rapidin
Echar un polvo

SEXTRAS

Una mamada
La paja
La frottage
Una carrera de pajas
Una margarita
La trastienda

El buceo
Un beso blanco
El beso negro
La lluvia dorada
Sesenta y nueve

BODY PARTY

Concha
Coño
Campana
Verga
Pito
Pinga
Huevos
Bolas
Tetas
Chichis
Culo

SEX POSITIONS

El misionero
Perrito
Cabalgando
Cabalgando hacia atras
La gran carretilla
En caja
El candelabro

SEX MOVES

Lama
Come
Toca
Agarra
Juega con
Manotea
Afeita
Pega
Saca

SEXUAL RELATIONSHIPS

Esposo/a
Novio/a
Amigovio/a
Tragon/a
Consuelo sexual
Amante
Mujeriego
Zorra
Puta
Prostituta
Virgen

Person 1: _____

Person 2: _____

Un día, _____ va a la casa de _____.

        (person 1)   *(person 2)*

_____ dice, "Hola _____. ¿Quieres _____?"

    (person 1)   *(sexual relationship)*   *(fuck word)*

_____ responde, "Hola _____. No, gracias. Quiero _____."

    (person 2)   *(sexual relationship)*   *(sextra)*

_____ va a _____ and _____ su _____.

    (person 1)   *(place)*   *(sexy move)*   *(body part)*

_____ dice, "Mmmm me gusta tu _____.

    (person 2)   *(body part)*

Ahora _____ mi _____."

    (sexy move)   *(body part)*

_____ dice, "No, quiero hacer _____ con tu _____.

    (person 1)   *(sextra)*   *(body part)*

_____ _____ su _____ y dice,

    (person 2)   *(sexy move)*   *(body part)*

"_____ me."

    (sexy move)

_____ dice, "Mmm, me gusta como tú _____.

    (person 1)   *(2nd person verb)*

Quiero _____ en _____."

    (fuck word)   *(sex position)*

_____ agarra su _____ y _____ lo como loco.

    (person 2)   *(body part)*   *(fuck word)*

_____ dice "¡Que _____ increíble! Tú eres un/una _____ bueno/a."

    (persona 1)   *(sextra)*   *(sexual relationship)*

CHAPTER 5

ANGRY SPANISH
ESPAÑOL ENCABRONADO

In hot-blooded, machismo-driven Latino culture, people get into it. I mean, they really get into it. In fact, cussing people out is kind of an art form. So if you wanna blend in and not look like the ignorant, pale-faced tourist that you probably are, you best quit being a bitch and get to learning some real shit talk, motherfucker.

•••••Gettin' pissed

It's important to be able to let someone know when they're pushing your buttons. Otherwise, how else will they know that you're about to go Samuel L. all over their asses?

SLANG BOX

ADJECTIVES

Angry/mad	*Enojado/a*
Pissed	*Encabronado/a*
Furious	*Furioso/a*
Gets on my nerves	*Me pone de los nervios*

VERBS

Annoys me	*Me molesta*
Ticks me off	*Me pone del hígado*

EXPRESSIONS

I'm getting angry.	*Me estoy enojando/a.*
I'm getting pissed off.	*Me estoy encabronando/a.*
I'm getting furious.	*Me estoy poniendo furioso.*
I'm about to lose it.	*Estoy a punto de perderlo.*
I'm gonna snap.	*Voy a soltar la rabia.*
Shut up!	*¡Cállate!*
I don't care.	*Me da igual.*
Leave me alone.	*Déjame en paz.*
Get away from me.	*Lárgate.*

Exercise 5.1 A   Angry adjectives

In Spanish, adjectives change depending on the number and gender of the people they describe. So a fat boy would be a chico gordo, *but a fat girl would be a* chica gorda. *Two fat boys would be* chicos gordos *and two fat chicks would be* chicas gordas. *And if there's a mixture of male and female fatties, Spanish always defaults to the masculine:* chicos gordos, *which seems kinda shitty for a chunkette who probably already suffers from low self-esteem without being called a dude.*

Write in the correct form of the adjectives in the blanks below. Pay attention to the gender and number of subjects in the sentence.

1. Maria is **furious** because her boyfriend keeps getting hand jobs from transvestites.

    Maria está _____ porque su novio sigue recibiendo pajas de travestis.

2. Carlos and I are **pissed** because the hookers never showed.

    Carlos y yo estamos _____ porque las prostitutas nunca llegaron.

3. Those girls are just **mad** because they can't get any dick.

    Esas chicas solamente están _____ porque no pueden conseguir la verga.

4. Diego gets **pissed off** when you check out his sister's tits.

    Diego se pone _____ cuando echas un vistazo a las tetas de su hermana.

5. I get **furious** if I can't use a dildo during sex.

    Me pongo _____ si no puedo usar un consolador durante sexo.

6. Those dudes are just **angry** 'cuz they got little dicks.

    Esos tipos solamente están _____ porque tienen cacahuates.

7. Why is she so **pissed**?

    ¿Por qué está ella tan _____?

Exercise 5.1 B Angry adjectives

Make your own sentence about why this person is pissed based on the picture below. BTW, the word for "condom" is condón.

Exercise 5.2 Anger management quiz

Choose the answer that best fits you, then read on to find out what the fuck your problem is.

1. Voy a soltar la rabia cuando…
    a. *mi madre está en mi casa.*
    b. *mi novio/a habla con otros chicos/chicas.*
    c. *mis amigos no me invitan a una fiesta.*
    d. *yo no recibo un aumento de sueldo (pay raise).*

2. Yo respondo, "Cállate y déjame en paz" cuando…
    a. *mi madre habla mucho.*
    b. *mi novio/a quiere sexo.*
    c. *mis amigos no hacen lo que quiero (don't do what I want).*
    d. *tengo mucho trabajo y mis compañeros hablan conmigo.*

3. Estoy a punto de perderlo cuando…
    a. *mi madre me da consejos (gives me advice).*
    b. *mi novio/a mira a otro chico/a.*
    c. *mis amigos hablan de mi.*
    d. *mi jefe me da mucho trabajo.*

4. Estoy encabronado/a cuando…

   a. *mi mamá viene a visitarme.*

   b. *mi novio/a no viene a mi casa.*

   c. *mis amigos no vienen a mi casa.*

   d. *tengo trabajo de casa.*

5. Quiero decir, "Lárgate" cuando…

   a. *mi mamá quiere verme.*

   b. *mi novio/a tiene otros planes.*

   c. *mis amigos tienen otros planes.*

   d. *mi jefe habla conmigo.*

ANSWER KEY

If you chose mostly "**a**" answers, you have a fucked-up relationship with your mother.

If you chose mostly "**b**" answers, you have some serious jealousy issues and your relationship probably sucks. If your partner hasn't dumped you yet, they soon will.

If you chose mostly "**c**" answers, you either need to chill out or find some better friends.

If you chose mostly "**d**" answers, your job eats it and you should quit.

Exercise 5.3   You're ticking me off!

Translate the conversation below into the speech bubbles of the drawings.

You: ¿Qué pasa?

Frat boy: Estoy encabronado porque eres un idiota.

You: ¿Qué? Déjame en paz.

Frat boy: No. Me molestas.

You: Cállate. Me estoy enojando.

Frat boy: Me da igual.

You: Me pones del hígado. Lárgate o voy a soltar la rabia.

Frat boy: Vámonos.

You: ¿Te gusta eso?

·····Fuck you

In Spanish, "fuck" isn't used as frequently as an insult or exclamation as it is in English. Spanish speakers generally just use it to refer to the act of fucking. That being said, there are more than enough ways of getting across the "fuck you" mentality. Adding the word for "shit" (*mierda*) or "I shit on" (*me cago*) usually gets across the extra punch that "fuck" adds in English.

SLANG BOX

EXPRESSIONS

Fuck!	*Coño!*	No fucking way.	*No hay manera de mierda.*
Fuck you.	*Chíngate.*		
I shit on you.	*Me cago en ti.*	Fuck that!	*¡A la mierda!*
Fuck your mother.	*Chinga tu madre.*	Don't fuck with me.	*No me chingues.*
I shit on your mother.	*Me cago en tu madre.*	You fucked up.	*La cagaste.*
Fuck off!	*¡Vete a la mierda!*	Fuck the whore of a mother who gave birth to you.	*Me cago en la puta madre que te parió.*
Go fuck yourself!	*¡Vete a la chingada!*		

Exercise 5.4   Punch it the fuck up

*Add the Spanish word for "shit" (*mierda*) to punch up the following phrases Spanish-style.*

1. *Vete.* (Go away)

    ¡Vete a la _____! (Go the fuck away!)

2. *Ninguna manera.* (No way)

    No hay manera de _____. (No fucking way!)

3. *Llegamos a un mal estado.* (We got messed up)

    Llegamos hasta la _____. (We got fucked up!)

4. *No me importa.* (I don't care)

    No me importa una _____. (I don't give a fuck!)

Exercise 5.5 I shit on you

Saying that you "shit on" something (me cago) in Spanish is the equivalent of saying "fuck it" in English. Choose people from the box below or add your own to tell us what you "shit on."

Your mom	*Tu madre*	**George Bush**	*Jorge Bush*
My boss	*Mi jefe*	**You**	*Ti*
That guy	*Ese tipo*		

1. Me cago en _____.

2. Me cago en _____.

3. Me cago en _____.

4. Me cago en _____.

5. Me cago en _____.

Exercise 5.6 Like it? Or shit on it?

Circle the appropriate category for each corresponding person or thing.

1. Mi novio/a   *¿Cago o Gusto?*

2. Mi trabajo   *¿Cago o Gusto?*

3. El presidente   *¿Cago o Gusto?*

4. Programas de realidad (*reality TV shows*)   *¿Cago o Gusto?*

5. Hombres   *¿Cago o Gusto?*

6. Mujeres   *¿Cago o Gusto?*

7. Los democrats   *¿Cago o Gusto?*

8. Los republicans   *¿Cago o Gusto?*

9. Donald Trump   *¿Cago o Gusto?*

10. Mis padres   *¿Cago o Gusto?*

·····Insults

Spanish insults are a thing of beauty. And Spanish speakers aren't afraid to use them. If you keep your ears open you'll be sure to hear all sorts of colorful little gems thrown around. One of my personal favorites—*tortillera*, Spanish slang for "dyke" but literally meaning "tortilla maker," which if you think about a couple of tortillas slapping together really begins to make sense. Defaming someone's intelligence is a classic first move in the insult game. So let us begin our lesson here.

SLANG BOX

NOUNS

Dummy	*Un/a bobo*	**Moron**	*Un/a tonto*
Dumbass	*Un/a gilún*	**Nitwit**	*Un/a baboso*
Dumbfuck	*Un/a gilazo*	**Halfwit**	*Un/a tarado*
Blockhead	*Un/a mendrugo*	**Retard**	*Un/a retardado*
Scatterbrain	*Un/a cabeza de chorlito*	**Mongoloid**	*Un/a mogólico*

Exercise 5.7 Unscramble the Scatterbrain

Unscramble and translate the following insults from Spanish to English:

1. nlúgi _____   *Translation:* _____

2. saoobb _____   *Translation:* _____

3. lcomignóo _____   *Translation:* _____

4. zgoila _____   *Translation:* _____

5. oobb _____   *Translation:* _____

6. dorata _____   *Translation:* _____

7. nemgudro _____   *Translation:* _____

8. oontt _____   *Translation:* _____

Exercise 5.8 Drawing for dummies

Use your newfound insult vocabulary to draw the following situation en español:

Tú estás encabronando porque un gilún te dice, "Me cago en tu madre."

Exercise 5.9 Don't be a dumbass

Use your newfound insult vocabulary to describe the situation pictured below:

_____

_____

_____

Exercise 5.10   Find the dumbfuck

Circle the following words for "dumbass" in Spanish below. Accents have been omitted.

Bobo

Chorlito

Gilazo

Mendrugo

Mogólico

Tarada

```
A   M   A   E   F   L   C   H   C
Y   O   V   N   A   N   H   T   H
B   G   G   X   D   A   F   Y   O
O   O   Y   U   A   O   E   Q   R
B   L   H   S   R   U   H   P   L
O   I   W   I   A   D   H   S   I
A   C   U   G   T   Z   N   T   T
U   O   A   Z   F   L   Y   E   O
O   Z   A   L   I   G   Z   U   M
```

Exercise 5.11 A   True or False

Choose verdadero *(true) or* falso *(false) for the following statements.*

1. Paris Hilton no es una tarada.   *¿Verdadero o falso?*

2. Barack Obama es un bobo.   *¿Verdadero o falso?*

3. Homer Simpson es un gilazo.   *¿Verdadero o falso?*

4. Bill Gates no es un baboso.   *¿Verdadero o falso?*

5. Jesús es un mendrugo.   *¿Verdadero o falso?*

6. Einstein es un gilún.   *¿Verdadero o falso?*

7. Mi padre no es un tonto.   *¿Verdadero o falso?*

8. Yo soy un/a mogólico.   *¿Verdadero o falso?*

9. Mi mamá es una cabeza de chorlito.   *¿Verdadero o falso?*

Exercise 5.11 B   Create your own

1. _____ es una tarada.

2. _____ es un bobo.

3. _____ es un gilazo.

4. _____ es un baboso.

5. _____ es un mendrugo.

6. _____ es una giluna.

7. _____ es un tonto.

8. _____ es un mogólico.

9. _____ es una cabeza de chorlito.

·····Biatch

Yes, there's a double standard for women. If men bang a bunch of broads, they're players. But if women fuck a lot of dudes, they're sluts. But when was the last time you heard a woman called a dickhead? Or how 'bout a douchebag? It works both ways, bitches!

SLANG BOX

NOUNS

Bitch	*Puta/perra*	Trick	*Furcia*
Slut	*Zorra*	Skank	*Macarra*
Whore	*Puta*	Hoochie	*Guarra*
Hooker	*Fulana*	Dyke	*Tortillera*
Tramp	*Mujerzuela*		

Exercise 5.12   Don't label me, bitch!

Label each woman pictured below with the correct derogatory term.

1. _____   2. _____   3. _____   4. _____

Exercise 5.13   You be the judge

Circle the answer you feel is correct.

1. **Martha Washington / Paris Hilton** es una zorra.

2. Mi mamá es una buena **persona / puta**.

3. Yo prefiero tener sexo con **virgenes / fulanas**.

4. Julia Roberts en *Pretty Woman* es una **guarra / furcia**.

5. **Eleanor Roosevelt / Monica Lewinsky** es una mujerzuela.

6. **Macarras / Rubias** se divierten más (*have more fun*).

7. Fulanas **aceptan dinero para sexo / comen mucho brócoli**.

8. Los politicos les gusta tener sexo con sus **esposas / furcias**.

9. Cuando yo soy mayor (*older*), yo quiero ser **el presidente / una zorra**.

10. **Rosa Parks / Rosie O'Donnell** es una tortillera.

Exercise 5.14   Match that slut!

Draw a line between the character and the description of what that character does. There may be more than one correct answer, and you may have to use some of the vocabulary you learned in the Horny Spanish chapter.

1. Perra

2. Zorra

3. Puta

4. Fulana

5. Mujerzuela

6. Furcia

7. Macarra

8. Guarra

9. Tortillera

a. Come la concha

b. Culea con cuatro hombres en una noche

c. Duerme con cualquier persona

d. Toma dinero para el sexo

e. Tiene sexo en el culo

f. Tiene sexo en la primera cita (*first date*)

g. Besa mujeres

h. Nunca está feliz

i. Le gusta el semen en su boca

·····Assholes!

Just as we have our own specialized insults for women, we have a whole lexicon for douches—I mean, dudes.

SLANG BOX

NOUNS

Son of a bitch	*Hijo de puta*	**Cocksucker**	*Mamavergas*
Sunnavabitch	*Hijueputa*	**Dickhead**	*Gilipollas*
Asshole	*Cabrón*	**Dipshit**	*Pendejo*
Motherfucker	*Malparido*	**Faggot**	*Maricón*

Exercise 5.15   Assholes and opinions

You know how they say that everyone has an asshole and an opinion? Well now you get to make opinions about assholes. Circle the answer that you feel is correct.

1.   **John F. Kennedy / Osama Bin Laden** es un hijueputa.

2.   Frat boys son **mamavergas / chicos inteligentes**.

3.   **Skaters / goths** son cabrones.

4.   Mi papá es un **gilipollas / buen hombre**.

5.   **Gandhi / Hitler** es un malparido.

6.   **Elton John / Ernest Hemingway** es un maricón.

7.   Los Republicans son **mamavergas / pendejos**.

8.   Mi jefe es un **gilipollas / maricón**.

Exercise 5.16   You better check yo'self before you wreck yo'self

Put a check in the box showing what each person would do.

	Acepta dinero para sexo	Chupa la verga	Duerme con muchos hombres	Duerme con la amiga de su esposa	Culea con dos hombres a la vez	Roba dinero de su amigo	Mama la panocha
Mujerzuela							
Mamavergas							
Perra							
Fulana							
Gilipollas							
Hjueputa							
Maricón							
Tortillera							

Exercise 5.17 Super insults

To punch up your insults you'll probably need a few handy adjectives to bandy about, because it's way more satisfying to call someone a fat, ugly fucker than just a fucker. Remember, adjectives always come after the noun and are specific to the gender and quantity of things being described.

ADJECTIVES		ADVERB	
Fat	*Gordo*	Fucking	*Pinche* (as in "fucking asshole"; *pinche* always comes before the noun)
Ugly	*Feo*		
Disgusting	*Asqueroso*		
Dumb	*Tonto*		
Skinny	*Flaco*		
Dirty	*Sucio*		

Using the words from the list above and any other insults you've learned in this chapter, translate the following sentences from English to Spanish:

1. You are a disgusting motherfucker!

   _____

2. Your mom is a skinny, dumb bitch.

   _____

3. Fuck you, you fucking dirty tramp.

   _____

4. Shut up, you skinny dyke whore.

   _____

5. Fuck off, you fucking faggot.

   _____

6. Your girlfriend is a dumb, dirty slut.

   _____

Make your own!

7. _____

_____

8. _____

_____

9. _____

_____

10. _____

_____

•••••Fightin' words

When push comes to shove, you gotta be ready to throw down and knock some bitches out…or at least shout the right words of encouragement to the badass Mexican *lucha libre* fighters who make our WWF wrestlers look like a bunch of oiled-up pussyboys.

SLANG BOX

VERBS

To fight	*Luchar*	To knock to pieces	*Reventar*
To beat the crap out of	*Dar una paliza*	To break	*Romper*
To whoop	*Batir*	To beat	*Golpear*
To destroy	*Hacer polvo*		

Exercise 5.18   Angry conjugation

A. *Since we usually talk about beat downs in the past tense, conjugate the -ar verbs below in the past using the model below to guide you. Then translate the example sentences into Spanish.*

To hook up

<u>I hooked up</u> with your sister.

<u>You hooked up</u> with your sister.

<u>He/She hooked up</u> with your sister.

<u>We hooked up</u> with your sister.

<u>They hooked up</u> with your sister.

Ligar

*Lig**ué** con tu hermana.*

*Lig**aste** con tu hermana.*

*Lig**ó** con tu hermana.*

*Lig**amos** con tu hermana.*

*Lig**aron** con tu hermana.*

To beat the crap out of

1. I beat the crap out of

2. You beat the crap out of

3. He/She beat the crap out of

4. We beat the crap out of

5. They beat the crap out of

6. He beat the crap out of that fat asshole!

_____

7. My sister beat the crap out of a dirty tramp last night!

_____

Dar una paliza

_____

_____

_____

_____

_____

B. *You conjugate both -ir and -er verbs in the past tense like this:*

To bone

<u>I boned</u> your mom.

<u>You boned</u> your mom.

<u>He/She boned</u> your mom.

<u>We boned</u> your mom.

<u>They boned</u> your mom.

Joder

*Jod**í** a tu madre.*

*Jod**iste** a tu madre.*

*Jod**ió** a tu madre.*

*Jod**imos** a tu madre.*

*Jod**ieron** a tu madre.*

To whoop   *Batir*

1. I whooped   _____

2. You whooped   _____

3. He/She whooped   _____

4. We whooped   _____

5. They whooped   _____

6. He whooped you like a little girl!

_____

7. I'm going to whoop your ass, bitch!

_____

C. *To conjugate "would" verbs (e.g., he would destroy you), you simply throw an –ía suffix at the end of the verb like this:*

To whoop   *Batir*

I would whoop you.   *Te batir**ía**.*

You would whoop me.   *Me batir**ías**.*

He/She would whoop you.   *Te batir**ía**.*

We would whoop you.   *Te batir**íamos**.*

They would whoop you.   *Te batir**ían**.*

To beat   *Golpear*

1. I would beat   _____

2. You would beat   _____

3. He/She would beat   _____

4. We would beat   _____

5. They would beat   _____

6. I would beat you like a rug (*alfombrilla*).

_____

7. He would beat you like a child.

_____

Exercise 5.19   Call it like you see it

Using the terms you have learned from this chapter, write one sentence in Spanish describing each picture below.

1.

_____

_____

_____

2.

_____

_____

_____

3.

_____

_____

_____

Exercise 5.20 Celebrity death match

Ever wonder who would win in a fight between Captain America and Captain Planet? No? Just me? That's cool. Well, now you can help me settle this long-running debate. Using your new fighting vocabulary and what you just learned about "would" verbs on page 107, write a sentence telling who would beat the crap out of whom or who would knock who to pieces for each of the matchups below.

Dar una paliza	*Reventar*
Batir	*Romper*
Hacer polvo	*Golpear*

(To make *hacer* a "would" verb, it becomes *yo haría, tú harías, él/ella haría, nosotros haríamos, ellos harían.*)

Example:

Albert Einstein vs. Thomas Edison: *Einstein rompería a Edison!*

1. She-Ra vs. Wonder Woman: _____

2. Scooby Doo vs. Lassie: _____

3. Superman vs. Jesus: _____

4. Gandhi vs. Martin Luther King Jr.: _____

5. Garfield vs. Winnie the Pooh: _____

6. George Washington vs. Abraham Lincoln: _____

7. Joan of Arc vs. Oprah: _____

8. The Golden Girls vs. The Spice Girls: _____

9. Screech vs. Urkel: _____

10. Mighty Morphin Power Rangers vs. Teenage Mutant Ninja Turtles: _____

Exercise 5.21   Kicks and punches

Sometimes you gotta break down the fight in detail when you describe it to your friends the next day. It's nice to know who won, but what's really important is describing how that crazy bitch got her weave ripped out.

SLANG BOX

NOUNS

A punch	*Un puñetazo*	**An uppercut**	*Un ganchazo*
A kick	*Una patada*	**A karate chop**	*Un hachazo de karate*
A backhand	*Un sopapo trasero*		
A slap	*Un guantazo*	**A headlock**	*Una llave de cabeza*
A smack	*Un golpe*	**A pile driver**	*Un martinete*

If you wanna use the words above as verbs, simply use the word dar *(to give). In Spanish, you wouldn't say, "She backhanded him," you would say, "She gave him a backhand" (*Le dio una sopapo trasero*). And if you wanted to say, "Uppercut him!" you would say, "Give him an uppercut!" (*¡Dale un ganchazo!*). So you need to get familiar with the word* dar. *Let's practice.*

To give	*Dar*	**Give!**	*¡Da!*
I gave	*Di*	**I smacked**	*Di un golpe*
You gave	*Diste*	**You smacked**	*Diste un golpe*
He/She gave	*Dio*	**He/She smacked**	*Dio un golpe*
We gave	*Dimos*	**We smacked**	*Dimos un golpe*
They gave	*Dieron*	**They smacked**	*Dieron un golpe*

And finally, use these pronouns to describe who you're smacking.

Me	*Me*	**I smacked him.**	*Le di un golpe.*
You	*Te*	**You smacked me.**	*Me diste un golpe.*
Him/Her	*Le*	**He smacked you.**	*Te dio un golpe.*
Us	*Nos*	**We smacked them.**	*Les dimos un golpe.*
Them	*Les*	**They smacked us.**	*Nos dieron un golpe.*
		Smack him!	*¡Dale un golpe!*

Now it's your turn. Translate the following sentences.

1. I karate chopped him!

_____

2. You kicked me in the dick!

_____

3. She slapped him!

_____

4. We backhanded them!

_____

5. Punch him in the balls!

_____

Exercise 5.22   My kung-fu is stronger than yours

The word for enemy in Spanish is enemigo. _Choose the best answer that tells how each person fights his_ enemigos.

1. Bruce Lee...

    a. les da guantazos a sus enemigos.

    b. pone sus enemigos en llaves de cabeza.

    c. les da hachazos de karate a sus enemigos.

2. Mike Tyson...

    a. les da ganchazos a sus enemigos.

    b. les da sopapos traseros a sus enemigos.

    c. les da hachazos de karate a sus enemigos.

3. Hulk Hogan...

    a. les da guantazos a sus enemigos.

    b. hace el martinete a sus enemigos.

    c. les da hachazos de karate a sus enemigos.

4. Un chulo (_a pimp_)...

    a. les da ganchazos a sus putas.

    b. pone sus putas en llaves de cabeza.

    c. les da sopapos traseros a sus putas.

5. Los gays...

    a. les dan guantazos a sus enemigos.

    b. ponen sus enemigos en llaves de cabeza.

    c. les dan hachazos de karate a sus enemigos.

6. Randy "Macho Man" Savage...

    a. les da ganchazos a sus enemigos.

    b. pone sus enemigos en llaves de cabeza.

    c. les da sopapos traseros a sus enemigos.

7. Muhammad Ali...

    a. les dan puñetazos a sus enemigos.

    b. hace el martinete a sus enemigos.

    c. les da hachazos de karate a sus enemigos.

Exercise 5.23　Label that pic!

Label each badass fight pic you see.

1. _____

2. _____

3. _____

4. _____

5. _____

6. _____

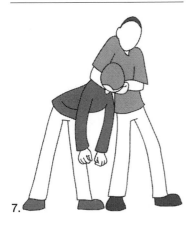

7. _____

8. _____

Exercise 5.24   Mix-n-match

Kicks and Punches	Bitches and Assholes	Flair
Un puñetazo	Hijueputa	Gordo
Una patada	Cabrón	Feo
Un sopapo trasero	Malparido	Asqueroso
Un guantazo	Mamavergas	Tonto
Un golpe	Gilipollas	Flaco
Un ganchazo	Pendejo	Sucio
Un hachazo de karate	Maricón	Pinche
Una llave de cabeza	Puta / Perra	
Un martinete	Zorra	
	Puta	
	Fulana	
	Mujerzuela	
	Furcia	
	Macarra	
	Guarra	
	Tortillera	

First, write your name and nine of your best friends, family members, or celebrities in the boxes labeled "People." Then select your favorite words from the list above to fill in the appropriate boxes below (refer back to the Horny Spanish chapter if you need a refresher on dirty body parts). Don't read across the rows until everything is filled in. Once you've filled everything in, read across the row and translate for instant hilarity. Did you know that Rainbow Bright smacked He-Man in the titty because he's a fat hooker?

Rainbow Bright + le da un golpe a + He Man + en la teta + porques es + una fulana + gordo.

People	Kicks and punches	People	Body part	Insult noun/mean name	Flair
Rainbow Bright	*un golpe*	He-Man	*la teta*	*una fulana*	*gordo*
(You)		(Friend 5)			
(Friend 1)		(Friend 6)			
(Friend 2)		(Friend 7)			
(Friend 3)		(Friend 8)			
(Friend 4)		(Friend 9)			

Exercise 5.25   Angry Scenarios

When traveling in foreign countries, you never know what kind of fucked-up situations you might get into. Maybe a gypsy tries to rob you. Maybe a bouncer throws you out of a bar. Maybe a customs officer finds the pound of heroin you've been muling through your asshole. Regardless of the kind of shit you get up to, it's important to be able to respond with the appropriate levels of anger required. Read the hypothetical situations below and choose the best response.

1. Situación número uno

So you're cruising down Las Ramblas in Barcelona with your girl when some mulleted Euro-douche checks out your girl's rack and says *¡Que tetas buenas!* You turn, slowly lock eyes with the punk and say:

    a. ¿Quieres tener sexo con ella?

    b. ¡Mi novia tiene una verga enorme!

    c. ¡Voy a darte una paliza!

    d. ¡Yo soy una zorra!

2. Situación número dos

You're walking through the crowded *zócalo* in Mexico checking out all the goods for sale, when you accidentally bump into some guy. He looks at you and says *¡Chíngate, pendejo!* You respond:

    a. ¡Soy un maricón encabronado!

    b. ¡No, chinga tu madre, cabrón!

    c. ¡Me encanta joder con mujerzuelas!

    d. ¿Cuál es tu número?

3. Situación número tres

You're touring Machu Picchu with your boyfriend and the tour guide won't stop looking at your man and feeling him up. While she's testing his biceps you step in and say:

    a. ¡Vete a la mierda, puta!

    b. Déjame en paz.

    c. ¿Te gusta reventar maricones?

    d. ¡Quiero culear contigo, tortillera!

4. Situación número cuatro

You're watching a soccer game at a bar in Argentina. One guy—a Brazil fan—won't shut up and keeps singing the Brazilian national anthem every time a player named Ronaldo touches the ball. Across the bar you shout at him:

    a. ¿Quieres echar un polvo en mi boca?

    b. ¡Voy a golpear una pinche furcia esta noche!

    c. ¡Cállate o voy a darte un sopapo trasero, malparido tonto!

    d. ¡Argentina es un país de tortilleras zorras!

5. Situación numero cinco

You've been waiting at a trendy restaurant in Bógota with some of your girlfriends for 30 minutes but the waitress keeps ignoring you while chatting up some greasy-looking dudes at the bar. You hand your purse to your friends and tell them:

    a. ¡Voy a soltar la rabia en la macarra sucia!

    b. ¡Los hombres son cabrones!

    c. ¡Ustedes son gilipollas!

    d. ¡Voy a hacer polvo de esos mamavergas gordos!

ANSWER KEY

Chapter One: Friendly Spanish

1.1

1.2 Answers may vary.
Acceptable answers for **1–5** are: Todo bien; Ando ahí nomás; Todo tranqui'; Como siempre; No mucho.
Acceptable answers for **6–1**- are: ¿Qué tal?; ¿Qué pasó?; ¿Qué haces?; ¿Qué dices?; ¿Quihubo?;
¿Cómo va todo?; ¿Cómo andas?; ¿Todo bien?

1.3 **1.** b, a, c **2.** c, b, a **3.** a, b, c **4.** c, a, b

1.4 **1.** a **2.** c **3.** c **4.** a or b **5.** a or b

1.5 **1.** b, d, f, e, c, a **2.** e, c, b, a, d **3.** c, a, e, b, d

1.6

1.7   Answers may vary.

1.8   1. Algún tipo 2. Mi comay 3. Amigote/a 4. Buena gente 5. Un chavo 6. Cole 7. Una chava
8. Mi compa 9. 'Mano 10. Nena 11. Chamaco 12. Los mucachos

1.9   1. a 2. b 3. c 4. a 5. c 6. b. 7. a

1.10 Answers may vary.

1.11

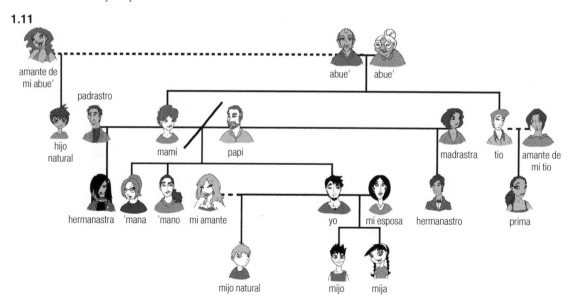

1.12 1. Abue' 2. Mami or vieja 3. Mami or vieja 4. 'mano 5. Tia 6. Amante 7. Tio or Papi or Tata or Viejo 8. Prima 9. Tio 10. Mami, vieja

1.13 Answers may vary but should include the following at the end of the response: 1. …Mijo/a 2. …'mano/a' 3. …papi/tata/mi Viejo/mami/mi vieja 4. Amante/mi media narnja 5. …media naranja/amante 6. …mijo/a 7. 'mano/a 8. …papi/tata/mi Viejo/a/mami 9. hijastro 10. …amante/media naranja.

1.14 Answers may vary.

1.15 Answers may vary.

1.16 Answers may vary.

1.17 Answers may vary.

Chapter Two: Party Spanish

2.1

```
S  B  O  B  A  W  R  M  G  F  L
W  O  F  A  G  N  A  B  B  Y  C
I  L  E  C  A  U  M  Y  L  U  P
U  I  S  A  N  P  E  V  R  A  N
J  C  T  N  T  K  R  Q  C  O  C
N  H  E  A  R  Z  I  H  T  Z  L
I  E  J  L  O  I  A  N  T  N  U
H  F  O  Q  M  N  E  G  T  E  B
A  V  N  F  G  V  E  Q  R  A  K
H  Z  Q  A  E  G  S  R  B  X  Q
P  N  I  R  O  J  Y  V  H  N  K
```

2.2 1. c 2. a 3. g 4. f 5. d 6. e 7. b

2.3 1. Pachanga 2. Fiesta paquete 3. Festejón 4. Antro, Ramería 5. Despedida de soltero, Antro de vicio

2.4 1. Estaba vacilando; Estabas vacilando; Estaba vacilando; Estabamos vacilando; Estaban vacilando 2. Estaba soltando una juerga; Estabas soltando una juerga; Estaba soltando una juerga; Estabamos soltando una juerga; Estaban soltando una juerga. 3. Estaba me deschavetando; Estabas te deschavetando; Estaba se deschavetando; Estabamos nos deschavetando; Estaban se deschavetando. 4. Ella estaba haciendo un perreo en mi verga. 5. El club estaba a toda madre. 6. Yo estaba me deschavetando en el antro de vicio.
7. Tu estabas gozando la pachanga. 8. Yo estaba haciendo un perreo en este culo!

2.5 Answers may vary.

2.6 1. Me 2. Se 3. Nos 4. Te 5. Se 6. Nos

2.7 1. Emboracharnos 2. Tragar algunos tragitos 3. Echar unas chelas; deschavetarnos 4. Traguitos 5. Emborracharme; cerveza; hacer un perreo 6. Trago 7. Un traguito y una cerveza 8. Cerveza; Salud

2.8 1. Una cerveza, una birra, and una chela are all appropriate answers 2. (una botella de) Mescal
3. Un traguito de tequila 4. Un vaso de sangria 5. Chicha

2.9 Answers may vary.

2.10 Answers may vary.

2.11

2.12 Answers may vary.

2.13 Answers may vary.

2.14 1. a 2. b 3. c 4. a 5. a

2.15

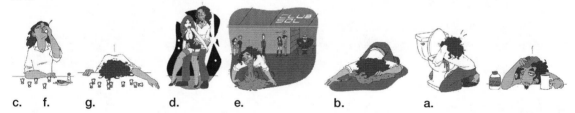

c.   f.   g.   d.   e.   b.   a.

2.16 1. c 2. b. 3. a. 4. c. 5. a. 6. b. 7. Answer may vary. 8. Answer may vary.

2.17

A	V	O	L	A	G	R	I	F	A
D	B	V	M	O	T	A	J	N	J
A	B	R	E	I	H	W	K	B	Y
F	B	L	F	U	M	E	R	O	L
W	B	M	O	D	A	G	O	R	D
H	P	V	I	W	W	Y	T	O	T
J	S	I	K	R	P	M	U	U	J
U	C	T	T	J	A	J	N	X	W
K	F	K	E	O	N	M	A	C	D
L	U	J	U	I	S	L	C	P	P

2.18 1. Perico; coke 2. Burundungas; roofies 3. Tacha; Ecstasy 4. Pastis; pills 5. Nieve; blow 6. Marimba; bud 7. Mota; weed

2.19 Answers may vary.

2.20 1. c 2. b 3. a 4. b 5. c 6. a

2.21 Answers may vary.

Chapter Three: Body Spanish

3.1 Answers may vary.

3.2 Answers may vary.

3.3 Answers may vary.

3.4 1. b 2. c 3. a 4. c 5. b

3.5 1. Gordinflónes Defeormes; 2. Nalgona or Culona; Fofita 3. Una buenota 4. Fornido; rico 5. Fofitos; fofos; 6. Palancónes; flacos

3.6 1. gordinflón 2. deforme 3. narigón 4. una buenota 5. fornido 6. jetón 7. palancón 8. nalgona or culona 9. fofita

3.7 1. Lamarlo 2. Lamarlo 3. Chingarlo 4. Lamarlo 5. Chingarlo 6. Chingarlo 7. Lamarlo 8. Chingarlo 9. Chingarlo 10. Lamarlo

3.8 1. Tetas; tits 2. Culo; ass 3. Pezones; nipples 4. Trasero 5. Chichis; titties 6. Ancas; ass cheeks 7. Globos; knockers 8. Bubis; boobies 9. Nalgona; big-booty ho (or big ass)

3.9 1. b; 2. c; 3. a; 4. c

3.10

P	P	B	C	O	L	A	Z	X	U
G	S	U	Z	S	S	F	V	G	Y
Y	Z	B	F	P	O	Y	A	K	O
M	U	I	I	E	B	N	Y	A	J
O	J	S	O	Z	O	G	E	I	N
L	J	V	N	O	L	U	S	S	A
U	Q	O	G	N	G	G	M	L	L
C	I	B	M	E	E	G	H	H	G
Q	N	C	N	S	O	I	I	Q	A
C	H	I	C	H	I	S	U	A	S

3.11 Answers may vary.

3.12 Answers may vary.

3.13

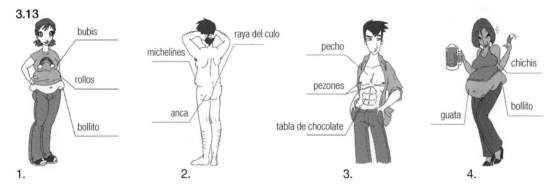

bubis

rollos

bollito

michelines

raya del culo

anca

pecho

pezones

tabla de chocolate

chichis

guata

bollito

1. 2. 3. 4.

3.14 Answers may vary.

3.15 Answers may vary.

3.16 1. Una cursera; mierda 2. Cagar; estreñido 3. Depositar un zurullo; mierda 4. Mear; cursera 5. Irme al trono; achicar la verga

3.17A 1. Yo cago; yo cagué 2. Tu cagas; tu cagaste 3. El/ella caga; el/ella cagó 4. Nosotros cagamos; nosotros cagamos 5. Ellos/ellas cagan; ellos/ellas cagaron 6. Necisito hacer una cagada! 7. Cagué mis pantalones. 8. Ella cagó un zurrullo enorme. 9. Mi novia comiu comida Indiana e cagó en la cama!

3.17B 1. Yo meo; yo mie 2. Tumeas; tu measte 3. El/ella mea; el/ella mearon 4. Nosotros meamos 5. Ellos mean; ellos mearon 6. Necisito mear 7. Me mie 8. Tu measte la cama.

Chapter Four: Horny Spanish

4.1 A 1. Enculo 2. Enculas 3. Encula 4. Enculamos 5. Enculan 6. Encular 7. Enculan 8. Enculan
      B 1. Cogo 2. Coges 3. Coge 4. Cogemos 5. Cogen 6. Cogo 7. Coges 8. Coge
      C 1. Cuelo 2. Culeas 3. Culea 4. Culeamos 5. Culean 6. Culeamos 7. Culear 8. Culea
      D 1. Jodo 2. Jodes 3. Jode 4. Jodemos 5. Joden 6. Joden 7. Jodo 8. Joder

4.2 1. The car 2. The shower 3. The bed 4. The floor 5. The pool

4.3 1. c. 2. c. 3. d. 4. c 5. d

4.4 1. Santa Claus culea con Señora Claus. 2. Answer may vary. 3. Snow White coge con el principe 4. Aladdin liga con la princesa Jasmin 5. Answer may vary.

4.5 1. Comeme 2. Lame me 3. Acaricia 4. Manotea 5. Agarra; lechea

4.6

```
N  N  Z  A  C  H  U  C  H  A
H  J  T  Z  H  U  E  V  O  S
K  I  K  J  H  U  M  F  E  P
G  T  A  H  C  N  O  C  W  U
Y  E  Z  M  A  B  S  C  T  N
V  D  A  L  M  B  F  O  Q  T
D  E  A  Z  P  O  B  Ñ  V  A
F  Z  R  W  A  L  B  O  W  D
W  U  N  G  N  A  O  W  R  A
E  L  Q  V  A  S  V  A  K  M
```

4.7 Answers may vary depending on the reader's drawing skills.

4.8 1. Chocha; poontang 2. Huevos; balls 3. Verga; cock 4. Concha; pussy 5. Puntada; boner 6. Campana; clit

4.9 1. c 2. b 3. a 4. d 5. a 6. Me gusta tu concha. 7. Mis huevos son grandes 8. ¿Quieres mi pito en tu concha? 9. Mi verga es mas grande que sus vergas. 10. Frota tu pinga en mi campana.

4.10 Answers may vary.

4.11 Answers may vary.

4.12 Answers may vary.

4.13 1. a. 2. b 3. c 4. a 5. a

4.14 Answers may vary depending on the reader's drawing skills.

4.15A 1. b 2. a 3. b 4. Answer may vary. 5. Answer may vary.

4.15B 1. Encima 2. En frente 3. Encima 4. En frente

4.16 1. b 2. c 3. a 4. c

4.17 Answers may vary.

4.18 Answers may vary depending on the reader's taste.

4.19 1. Amigovia 2. Pareja 3. Consuelo sexual 4. Liga 5. Prostitute 6. Amante 7. Virgin 8. Mujeriego; Zorra

4.20 Answers may vary.

4.21 Emilio: una; un Juan: un Emilio: una Juan: un; una; un Juan: una Emilio: un; una

4.22 1. f 2. c 3. h 4. b 5. g 6. d 7. a 8. e

4.23 Answers may vary.

Chapter Five: Angry Spanish

5.1A 1. Furiosa 2. Encabronados 3. Enojadas 4. Encabronado 5. Furioso/a 6. Enojados 7. Encabronada

5.1B Answer may vary.

5.2 Answers may vary.

5.3

5.4 1. Mierda 2. Mierda 3. Mierda 4. Mierda

5.5 Answers may vary.

5.6 Answers may vary.

5.7 1. Gilún; dumbass 2. Baboso; nitwit 3. Mogólico; mongloid 4. Gilazo; dumbfuck 5. Bobo; dummy 6. Tarado; halfwit 7. Mendrugo; blockhead 8. Tonto; moron

5.8 Answers may vary depending on the reader's drawing skills.

5.9 Answers may vary.

5.10

A	M	A	E	F	L	C	H	C
Y	O	V	N	A	N	H	T	H
B	G	G	X	D	A	F	Y	O
O	O	Y	U	A	O	E	Q	R
B	L	H	S	R	U	H	P	L
O	I	W	I	A	D	H	S	I
A	C	U	G	T	Z	N	T	T
U	O	A	Z	F	L	Y	E	O
O	Z	A	L	I	G	Z	U	M

5.11A Answers may vary.

5.11B Answers may vary.

5.12 1. Puta or perra 2. Tortillera 3. Fulana or puta 4. Guarra

5.13 Answers may vary.

5.14 Answers may vary.

5.15 Answers may vary.

5.16 Answers may vary.

5.17 Answers may vary.

5.18A 1. (Yo) di una paliza 2. (Tu) diste una paliza 3. (El/Ella) dio una paliza 4. (Nosotros) dimos una paliza 5. (Ellos/Ellas) dieron una paliza 6. El dio una paliza ese cabrón gordo 7. Mi hermana dio una paliza a una mujerzuela sucia anoche

5.18B 1. (Yo) batí 2. (Tu) batiste 3. (El/Ella) batió 4. (Nosotros) batimos 5. (Ellos/Ellas) batieron 6. El te batió como una nena 7. Voy a batir tu culo, puta!

5.18C 1. (Yo) golpearía 2. (Tu) golpearías 3. (El/Ella) golpearía 4. (Nosotros) golpearíamos 5. (Ellos/Ellas) golpearían 6. (Yo) te golpearía como una alfombrilla. 7. El te golpearía como un niño.

5.19 Answers may vary.

5.20 Answers may vary.

5.21 1. You le di un hachazo de karate! 2. Me diste una patada en el pito! 3. Ella le dio un guantazo! 4. Les dimos un sopapo trasero! 5. Dale un puñetazo en los huevos!

5.22 Answers may vary.

5.23 1. Un punetazo 2. Una patada 3. Un sopapo trasero 4. Un guantazo 5. Un ganchazo 6. Un golpe 7. Una llave de cabeza 8. Un martinete

5.24 Answers may vary.

5.25 1. c 2. b 3. a 4. c 5. a

•••••About the Author

NDB moved from the glorious taco-truck-lined streets of Oakland, California, to a Mexican food wasteland in the South in order to teach high school Spanish. He continues to live in the South and now works in education reform. Despite the paucity of good Mexican food there (or good any kind of food beside barbecue, really), NDB is strangely happy.